SENSATIONAL SPORTS TEAMS

Dodger Blue
THE LOS ANGELES DODGERS

David Aretha

MyReportLinks.com Books

an imprint of

 Enslow Publishers, Inc.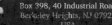

Box 398, 40 Industrial Road
Berkeley Heights, NJ 07922
USA

MyReportLinks.com Books, an imprint of Enslow Publishers, Inc. MyReportLinks®
is a registered trademark of Enslow Publishers, Inc.

Library of Congress Cataloging-in-Publication Data

Aretha, David.
  Dodger blue : the Los Angeles Dodgers / David Aretha.
    p. cm. — (Sensational sports teams)
  Includes bibliographical references and index.
  ISBN-13: 978-1-59845-045-3
  ISBN-10: 1-59845-045-X
  1. Los Angeles Dodgers (Baseball team)—Juvenile literature. 2. Los Angeles Dodgers (Baseball
team)—History—Juvenile literature. 3. Dodger Stadium (Los Angeles, Calif.)—Juvenile literature. I.
Title. II. Series.
  GV875.L6A74 2007
  796.357'640979494—dc22
                            2006019244

Printed in the United States of America

10 9 8 7 6 5 4 3 2 1

To Our Readers:
Through the purchase of this book, you and your library gain access to the Report Links that specifically
back up this book.
The Publisher will provide access to the Report Links that back up this book and will keep these Report
Links up to date on **www.myreportlinks.com** for five years from the book's first publication date.
We have done our best to make sure all Internet addresses in this book were active and appropriate when
we went to press. However, the author and the Publisher have no control over, and assume no liability
for, the material available on those Internet sites or on other Web sites they may link to.
The usage of the MyReportLinks.com Books Web site is subject to the terms and conditions stated on the
Usage Policy Statement on **www.myreportlinks.com.**
A password may be required to access the Report Links that back up this book. The password is found
on the bottom of page 4 of this book.
Any comments or suggestions can be sent by e-mail to comments@myreportlinks.com or to the address
on the back cover.

Photo Credits: AP/Wide World Photos, pp. 1, 3, 6, 10, 14, 20, 26, 30, 34–35, 44, 50–51, 60, 67, 70,
76, 78, 82, 84, 94, 98–99, 102, 104, 106, 108, 110, 112; Ballpark digest, p. 59; Baseball Almanac, p. 8;
BBC, p. 52; BaseballLibrary.com, p. 64; Carl Erskine c/o CMG Worldwide, p. 36; ESPN Internet Ventures,
p. 66; Estate of Jackie Robinson c/0 CMG Worldwide, p. 97; Exploratorium, p. 39; FunTrivia.com, p. 18;
Houston Chronicle, p. 24; Independent Television Service, p. 87; Library of Congress, p. 16;
LosAngelesDodgers Online.com, p. 62; *Los Angeles Times*, p. 111; MLB Advanced Media, L.P., pp. 80, 89,
90, 92; Munsey & Suppes, p. 40; MyReportLinks.com Books, p. 4; National Baseball Hall of Fame and
Museum, Inc., pp. 29, 72; O'Malley Seidler Partners, LLC, p. 77; Society For American Baseball Research,
p. 23; Tank Productions, p. 46; The Hardball Times, p. 58; *The New York Times*, p. 38; The Society For
American Baseball Research and The Respective Authors, p. 57; *The Sporting News* Online, p. 12; The
Washington Post Company, p. 32; *USA Today*, p. 54.

Cover Photo: AP/Wide World Photos

Contents

MyReportLinks.com Books
Great Books, Great Links, Great for Research!

The Internet sites featured in this book can save you hours of research time. These Internet sites—we call them **"Report Links"**—are constantly changing, but we keep them up to date on our Web site.

When you see this "Approved Web Site" logo, you will know that we are directing you to a great Internet site that will help you with your research.

Give it a try! Type http://www.myreportlinks.com into your browser, click on the series title and enter the password, then click on the book title, and scroll down to the Report Links listed for this book.

The Report Links will bring you to great source documents, photographs, and illustrations. MyReportLinks.com Books save you time, feature Report Links that are kept up to date, and make report writing easier than ever! A complete listing of the Report Links can be found on pages 114–115 at the back of the book.

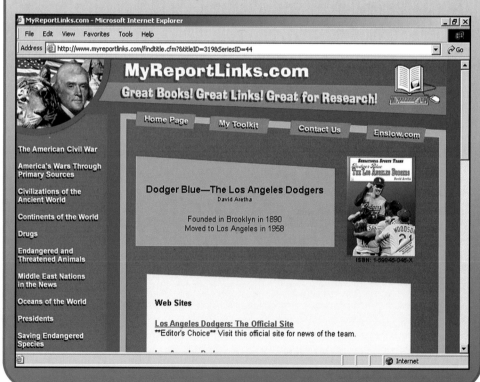

Please see "To Our Readers" on the copyright page for important information about this book, the MyReportLinks.com Web site, and the Report Links that back up this book.

Please enter **LAD1352** if asked for a password.

DODGER FACTS

➔ **Won World Series**
1955; 1959; 1963; 1965; 1981; 1988

➔ **Won NL Pennant but Not World Series**
1916; 1920; 1941; 1947; 1949; 1952–53; 1956; 1966; 1974; 1977–78

HOME FIELD	PLAYED THERE
Washington Park I (Brooklyn)	1890
Eastern Park (Brooklyn)	1891–97
Washington Park II (Brooklyn)	1898–1912
Ebbets Field (Brooklyn)	1913–57
Roosevelt Stadium (Jersey City, N.J.)	1957
Memorial Coliseum (Los Angeles)	1958–61
Dodger Stadium	1962–present

RETIRED NUMBERS	POSITION	YEARS
No. 1: Pee Wee Reese	Shortstop	1940–42; 1946–58
No. 2: Tommy Lasorda	Manager	1976–96
	Pitcher	1954–55
No. 4: Duke Snider	Center Field	1947–62
No. 19: Jim Gilliam	2B, 3B, and Outfield	1953–66
No. 20: Don Sutton	Pitcher	1966–80; 1988
No. 24: Walter Alston	Manager	1954–76
No. 32: Sandy Koufax	Pitcher	1955–65
No. 39: Roy Campanella	Catcher	1948–57
No. 42: Jackie Robinson	Second Base	1947–56
No. 53: Don Drysdale	Pitcher	1956–69

Kirk Gibson pumps his fist in triumph as he rounds the bases after his pinch-hit home run in Game 1 of the 1988 World Series.

"I Don't Believe What I Just Saw!"

 **1**

Kirk Gibson, slugger for the Los Angeles Dodgers, had never felt so helpless. Here he was, during Game 1 of the 1988 World Series, watching the game in the trainer's room. Half-dressed with an ice pack on his knee, Gibson had not swung a bat in three days. Inning after inning went by, with his Dodgers trailing the mighty Oakland A's, and all Gibson could do was stare at the television screen.

"I heard NBC's Vin Scully say, over and over, 'Gibson will not be playing tonight,'" Gibson wrote. " 'He's not even in the dugout.' Something about the finality of his words agitated me. My mind began rumbling. I was beginning to feel energy from the game. I visualized one final at-bat."[1]

Gibson told Mitch Poole, the clubhouse attendant, to set up the indoor batting tee and hitting net. Poole was dumbfounded. Everyone knew that with his injured left hamstring and sprained right knee, Gibson could barely stand up.

"What?" Poole asked.

"Set it up," Gibson urged. "Hurry!"[2]

Prior to the season, the Dodgers had signed Gibson as a free agent, hoping he would light a fire under the ballclub. A football star in college, Gibson brought a warrior's mentality to the diamond. For the Detroit Tigers in 1984, he blasted 2 home runs in Game 5 to clinch the World Series championship. Gibson earned the National League MVP award with Los Angeles in 1988—not just because of his 25 home runs, but also because of his commanding leadership.

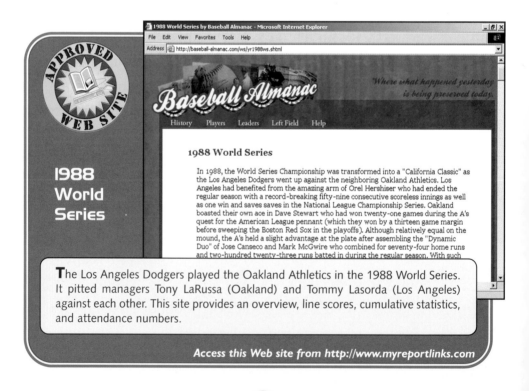

APPROVED WEB SITE

1988 World Series

1988 World Series by Baseball Almanac - Microsoft Internet Explorer

File   Edit   View   Favorites   Tools   Help

Address http://baseball-almanac.com/ws/yr1988ws.shtml

Baseball Almanac

Where what happened yesterday is being preserved today.

History   Players   Leaders   Left Field   Help

1988 World Series

In 1988, the World Series Championship was transformed into a "California Classic" as the Los Angeles Dodgers went up against the neighboring Oakland Athletics. Los Angeles had benefited from the amazing arm of Orel Hershiser who had ended the regular season with a record-breaking fifty-nine consecutive scoreless innings as well as one win and saves saves in the National League Championship Series. Oakland boasted their own ace in Dave Stewart who had won twenty-one games during the A's quest for the American League pennant (which they won by a thirteen game margin before sweeping the Boston Red Sox in the playoffs). Although relatively equal on the mound, the A's held a slight advantage at the plate after assembling the "Dynamic Duo" of Jose Canseco and Mark McGwire who combined for seventy-four home runs and two-hundred twenty-three runs batted in during the regular season. With such

The Los Angeles Dodgers played the Oakland Athletics in the 1988 World Series. It pitted managers Tony LaRussa (Oakland) and Tommy Lasorda (Los Angeles) against each other. This site provides an overview, line scores, cumulative statistics, and attendance numbers.

Access this Web site from http://www.myreportlinks.com

In the 1988 National League Championship Series, Gibson belted key home runs in two wins over the New York Mets. But Gibson pulled his left hamstring while stealing a base in Game 5. Then in Game 7, he sprained his right knee while trying to break up a double play.

The Dodgers desperately needed Gibson's firepower in the World Series. After all, they were facing the dominant Athletics, who had won 104 games and featured "Bash Brothers" Mark McGwire and Jose Canseco. Gibson tried to take batting practice during a pre-Series workout, but he quit after several minutes. The pain was too great. Prior to Game 1, Dr. Frank Jobe injected cortisone into Gibson's knee. However, Jobe was not sure if Gibby would play in any Series games at all.

Gibson missed the pregame introductions for Game 1 at Dodger Stadium. In the trainer's room, he cheered when his replacement in left field, Mickey Hatcher, launched a two-run homer in the first inning. In the second, however, Canseco socked a grand slam. Twice during the game, Dodgers manager Tommy Lasorda jogged from the dugout through the tunnel to ask Gibson if he could play. Both times Gibson gave him a thumbs-down.

Los Angeles scored in the sixth, and through eight innings Oakland led 4–3. The eighth inning is when Gibson had a change of heart. He sent Poole to get Lasorda.

Star pitcher Orel Hershiser is mobbed by his teammates as they celebrate their World Series victory over the Oakland Athletics.

"I'm trying to manage a World Series game here," Lasorda snapped back at Poole.

"Gibby wants to talk to you," Poole replied. "He wants to hit."[3]

Oakland entered the bottom of the ninth with a 4–3 lead and relief ace Dennis Eckersley on the mound. The crafty right-hander had enjoyed one of the greatest seasons ever for a closer, saving 45 games. Across America, fans wondered if the Dodgers' heart and soul would be available to pinch hit. But even when the bottom of ninth began, Gibson was still not in the dugout.

In full command, Eckersley made quick work of the Dodgers hitters. Mike Scioscia popped out to shortstop, and Jeff Hamilton took a called strike three. Mike Davis, a .196 hitter during the season, walked to the plate while light-hitting Dave Anderson entered the on-deck circle. Eckersley, who owned better control than any pitcher in baseball, surprisingly walked Davis. That brought up Anderson . . . but wait!

Anderson retreated to the dugout, and out came Gibson. Fifty-six thousand fans rose to their feet as he limped into the left batter's box. Wrote Gibson, "The pain became secondary to the deafening roar of the crowd."[4] Yet the injuries were clearly a handicap. On the first pitch, he fouled off a fastball with a feeble swing. He fouled the next pitch, too, falling behind 0–2.

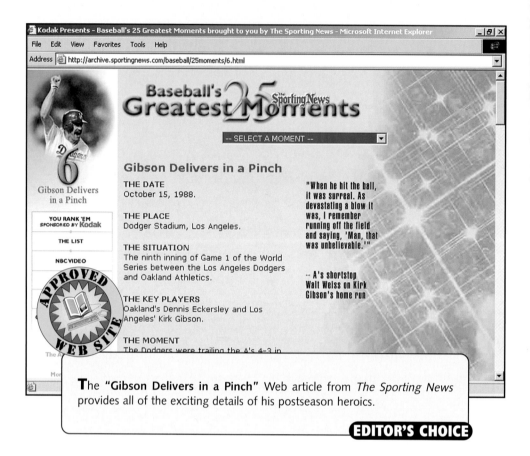

Baseball's 25 Greatest Moments
The Sporting News

-- SELECT A MOMENT --

Gibson Delivers in a Pinch

THE DATE
October 15, 1988.

THE PLACE
Dodger Stadium, Los Angeles.

THE SITUATION
The ninth inning of Game 1 of the World Series between the Los Angeles Dodgers and Oakland Athletics.

THE KEY PLAYERS
Oakland's Dennis Eckersley and Los Angeles' Kirk Gibson.

THE MOMENT
The Dodgers were trailing the A's 4–3 in

"When he hit the ball, it was surreal. As devastating a blow it was, I remember running off the field and saying, 'Man, that was unbelievable.'"

-- A's shortstop Walt Weiss on Kirk Gibson's home run

Gibson Delivers
in a Pinch

YOU RANK 'EM
SPONSORED BY **Kodak**

THE LIST

NBC VIDEO

APPROVED WEB SITE

The **"Gibson Delivers in a Pinch"** Web article from *The Sporting News* provides all of the exciting details of his postseason heroics.

EDITOR'S CHOICE

Gibson altered his stance, wanting just to put the ball in play. He chopped the next pitch foul, then took two pitches for balls. The count was 2–2. On the next delivery, also a ball, Davis stole second base. If Gibby could somehow smack a single on the 3–2 pitch, Davis would probably score the tying run.

At that moment, Gibson recalled what Dodgers scout Mel Didier had told him. On full-count pitches, Eckersley often threw a backdoor slider (a hard breaking ball that starts outside of the plate but comes back over the outer edge). Eckersley did indeed throw the backdoor slider, and Gibson —taking what he called an "ugly swing"[5]—flicked the ball skyward. "High fly ball into right field . . .," blared Scully. "She is . . . gone!"[6]

Pandemonium erupted. Fans jumped up and down, pounding their heads. Lasorda and his players bolted out of the dugout, arms raised triumphantly. Gibson, in a home run "hobble," pumped his fist twice as he rounded first base. Marveled radio announcer Jack Buck, "I don't believe what I just saw!"[7] Declared Scully, "In a year that has been so improbable, the impossible has happened!"[8]

Kirk Gibson would not play again in the entire Series, but it did not matter. Oakland could not bounce back from one of the most dramatic hits in the history of baseball. "That paralyzed the A's, just paralyzed them," said Lasorda. "They never, ever recovered. I can see it as if it was yesterday. They just stood in the field. They couldn't believe it."[9]

In a huge upset, the Dodgers went on to win the World Series in five games. Years later, fans in California voted Gibson's home run as the greatest moment in Los Angeles sports history.

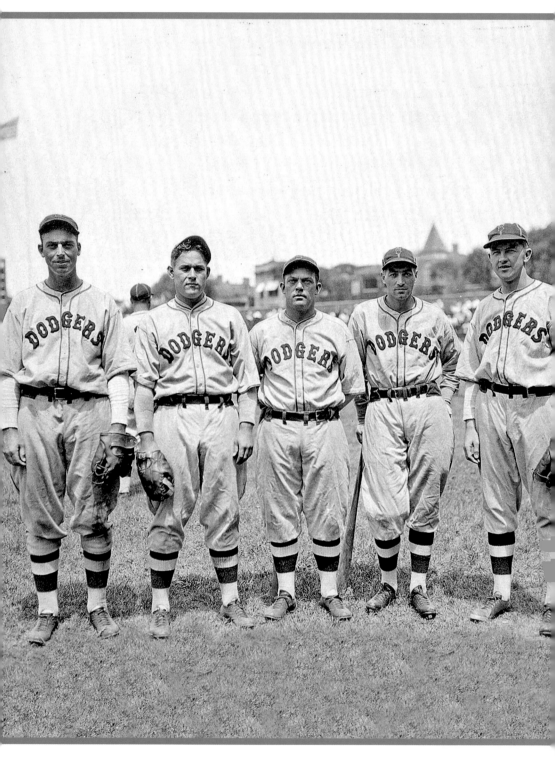

▲ *Members of the 1933 Dodgers line up for a photo. From left to right are Joe Hutcheson, Sam Leslie, Dan Taylor, Johnny Frederick, and Walter Beck.*

THE BUMS OF BROOKLYN

From an early age, children become aware of the Dodgers—one of the great teams in American sports history. Yet inevitably, in a moment of deep thought, the young tykes will turn to their parents and ask, "Mom, Dad . . . what's a dodger?"

The origin of "Dodgers" dates back to the 1890s in Brooklyn. Back then, fans of the team had difficulty getting to the ballfield since the streets were congested with trolley cars. Pedestrians on their way to Eastern Park, where the team played, had to "dodge" the trolleys. Thus, some people called the team the "Trolley Dodgers." Nevertheless, the evolution of the team's name is much more involved.

The ballclub actually took shape in 1884, in the American Association. Over the next few years, they were known as the Brooklyn Atlantics

and Brooklyn Grays. When the team joined the
National League (the same league that exists
today) in 1890, it was called the Brooklyn
Bridegrooms. Apparently, some of the players
had recently gotten married—hence the unusual
name. In their first year in the NL, the Bridegrooms
finished in first place.

In 1899, Brooklyn acquired several future Hall
of Famers from the Baltimore Orioles. The club
was so good that year (101–47) that they changed
their name to the Superbas, and stuck with it until
1910. They borrowed the name from a popular
Broadway musical of the time. Outfielder Willie
Keeler was the team's main attraction. Standing

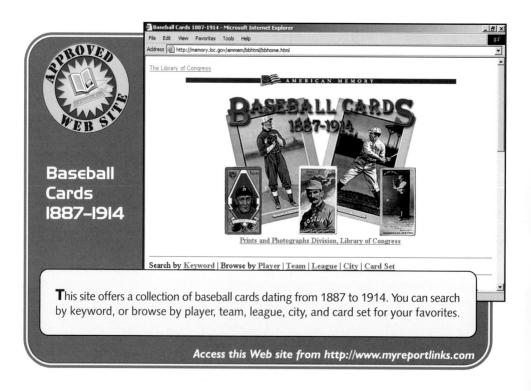

**Baseball
Cards
1887–1914**

This site offers a collection of baseball cards dating from 1887 to 1914. You can search
by keyword, or browse by player, team, league, city, and card set for your favorites.

Access this Web site from http://www.myreportlinks.com

just five feet four inches, "Wee Willie" excelled at bunting and hitting the ball where the fielders were not. "Hit 'em where they ain't," he advised.[1]

Charles Ebbets also became a local hero. Ebbets began his career with the team as a ticket taker in 1883, and by 1907 he became majority owner of the ballclub. But his Superbas by that time were no longer superb, and the team's ball field (Washington Park) was even worse. He worried that the wooden grandstands would collapse or catch fire. Ebbets decided that a grander ballpark would be built on a garbage dump called "Pigtown."

The Daffiness Boys

Ebbets Field opened in 1913, and a year later the jovial Wilbert Robinson took over as manager. Players and fans loved the new skipper, calling him "Uncle Robbie." In fact, they even changed the team name to the Brooklyn Robins in his honor. In 1916 and 1920, he led Brooklyn to its first two modern World Series—both losses. In Game 2 of the 1916 Series, the Robins lost in fourteen innings to the Boston Red Sox. Boston's Babe Ruth pitched shutout ball over the last thirteen frames.

Although Robinson's team did not make it back to the Series during the Roaring '20s, they kept fans amused. The players became known as the

"Daffiness Boys" for their airheaded blunders. An example: During a game on August 15, 1926, the Robins wound up with three runners at third base—at the same time! Outfielder Babe Herman was the daffiest of the Robins. Though he was a great hitter (he batted .393 in 1930), fly balls tended to bonk him in the head.

When Robinson stepped down as manager after the 1931 season, the name Robins no longer made sense. So in 1932, the team's longtime nickname, the Dodgers, became official—never to be changed again.

In the 1920s and 1930s, the New York Yankees and New York Giants frequently made the World

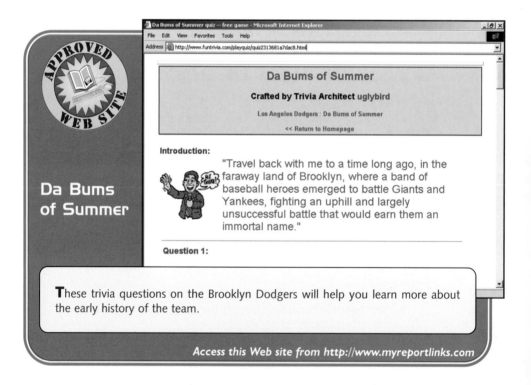

Da Bums of Summer

Da Bums of Summer quiz -- free game - Microsoft Internet Explorer

File Edit View Favorites Tools Help

Address http://www.funtrivia.com/playquiz/quiz2313681a7dac8.html

Da Bums of Summer

Crafted by Trivia Architect uglybird

Los Angeles Dodgers : Da Bums of Summer

<< Return to Homepage

Introduction:

"Travel back with me to a time long ago, in the faraway land of Brooklyn, where a band of baseball heroes emerged to battle Giants and Yankees, fighting an uphill and largely unsuccessful battle that would earn them an immortal name."

Question 1:

These trivia questions on the Brooklyn Dodgers will help you learn more about the early history of the team.

Access this Web site from http://www.myreportlinks.com

Series. But the Dodgers were perennial also-rans. In 1934, New York Giants manager Bill Terry cracked, "Is Brooklyn still in the league?"[2] One day that year, they were shut out twice in a double-header by St. Louis Cardinals pitchers (and brothers) Dizzy and Daffy Dean. Dodgers fans became so frustrated that they simply referred to their team as "Dem Bums."

Of course, the "Bums" had their occasional moments of glory. In 1932, Lefty O'Doul led the National League in batting with a .368 average. On May 14, 1933, stocky slugger Hack Wilson socked a pinch-hit, game-winning, inside-the-park grand slam. But the biggest moment of all came on a frigid January day in 1938, when Larry MacPhail was hired to rebuild the Dodgers.

The Innovator

When MacPhail interviewed for the job of team president, he told the Dodgers owners to hurry up and make up their minds because he had a train to catch. Once hired, this lawyer and World War I veteran gave the Dodgers an immediate makeover.

MacPhail had Ebbets Field repainted and the playing field redone; no longer would fielders be plagued by bad hops. The Yankees, Giants, and Dodgers previously had agreed not to broadcast games on the radio. But MacPhail broke the accord, and he hired the talented Red Barber to do

19

the radio play-by-play. MacPhail also installed lights in the stadium. During Ebbets Field's first night game, on June 15, 1938, Cincinnati's Johnny Vander Meer made history by throwing his second straight no-hitter.

△ "Leo the Lip" Durocher is considered to be one of the greatest managers in baseball history. Here he signs autographs for models who appeared in a fashion show before the Brooklyn Dodgers game on August 22, 1941.

MacPhail tried everything to bring fans to the ballpark. On August 2, he introduced yellow baseballs. In June, he hired forty-three-year-old Babe Ruth to coach first base. Fans packed Ebbets to watch the former Yankees legend blast "home runs" during batting practice. After the games, the Babe spent at least an hour signing autographs. He did not stop until every young fan went home happy. Although the Dodgers finished 69–80 in 1938, they attracted 180,000 more fans than the year before.

On August 26, 1939, MacPhail brought baseball to television. Red Barber hosted a Saturday afternoon game between Cincinnati and Brooklyn. Reported The *New York Times,* "Television set owners as far as fifty miles away viewed the action and heard the roar of the crowd."[3] In 1939 and 1940, the Dodgers acquired a pair of .300 hitters: Joe "Ducky" Medwick and Dixie "The People's Cherce" Walker. Exciting rookies Pee Wee Reese (a slick-fielding shortstop) and Pete Reiser (a dynamic outfielder) premiered in 1940.

MacPhail's Brooklyn Makeover

Under fiery manager Leo Durocher, the Dodgers won 100 games and the National League pennant in 1941. Reiser led the league in batting (.343), and Dolph Camilli paced the circuit in home runs (34). The city of New York was all abuzz as the

Dodgers faced the Yankees in a "Subway Series." Though the Yanks took two of the first three games, it appeared that Brooklyn would win the fourth game. However, with two outs in the ninth inning, Dodgers catcher Mickey Owen dropped a third strike. The Yankees batter reached first base on the play, and New York rallied to win. The Yankees won the series in five games—their first of eight world titles at the Dodgers' expense.

In 1942, the Dodgers won a team-record 104 games. Although they finished in second place, reporters marveled at MacPhail's accomplishments. In less than five years, he had refurbished the stadium and turned a losing team into a powerhouse. More than a million fans a season were packing Ebbets Field. He introduced radio, television, and night ball to Brooklyn. Moreover, he had made the Dodgers' minor-league system the envy of baseball. Yet in September 1942, MacPhail called it quits. The United States had entered World War II, and he was off to support his country.

The War Years

As war raged through 1945, some of the Dodgers joined the fight. Pee Wee Reese served in the Navy, while Pete Reiser joined the Army. Major League Baseball continued throughout the war, but the quality of play dipped to new lows. On April 27, 1944, Boston Braves knuckleball pitcher Jim Tobin

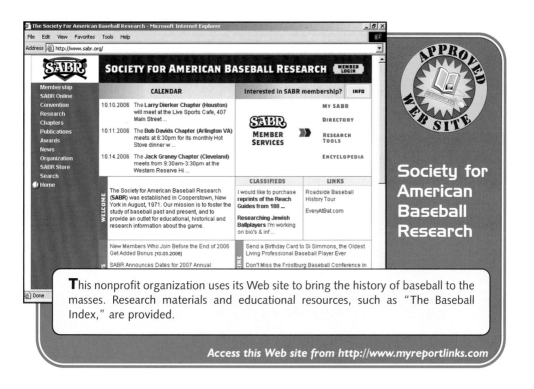

This nonprofit organization uses its Web site to bring the history of baseball to the masses. Research materials and educational resources, such as "The Baseball Index," are provided.

Access this Web site from http://www.myreportlinks.com

no-hit the Dodgers and hit a home run. Only 1,984 fans at Braves Field witnessed the feat. On August 20, 1945, Dodgers shortstop Tommy Brown—sixteen years old—became the youngest person ever to hit a home run in the major leagues.

The Dodgers did not contend for a pennant during the war years. However, in November 1942, they signed Branch Rickey to be their general manager. With St. Louis, Rickey had built the Cardinals into perennial title contenders. Rickey rivaled MacPhail as baseball's brightest mind, and in August 1945 he became part-owner of the Dodgers. At war's end, Rickey possessed the power, foresight, and courage to make the boldest decision in major-league history.

Breaking the Barrier

During World War II, many thousands of African Americans had served their country, fighting to defend American freedom. Yet through 1945, not a single African-American man had played major-league baseball in the twentieth century. The Negro Leagues thrived, but African Americans were in effect barred from the majors. Millions of Americans realized the injustice, but only Rickey had the determination to force a change.

Rickey realized that many of the best ballplayers in the country were Negro Leaguers. His plan was

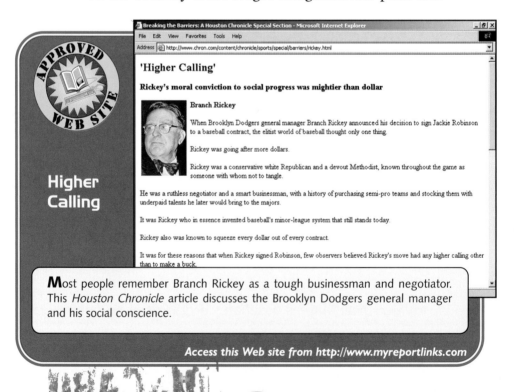

Higher Calling

Breaking the Barriers: A Houston Chronicle Special Section - Microsoft Internet Explorer

File   Edit   View   Favorites   Tools   Help

Address http://www.chron.com/content/chronicle/sports/special/barriers/rickey.html

'Higher Calling'

Rickey's moral conviction to social progress was mightier than dollar

Branch Rickey

When Brooklyn Dodgers general manager Branch Rickey announced his decision to sign Jackie Robinson to a baseball contract, the elitist world of baseball thought only one thing.

Rickey was going after more dollars.

Rickey was a conservative white Republican and a devout Methodist, known throughout the game as someone with whom not to tangle.

He was a ruthless negotiator and a smart businessman, with a history of purchasing semi-pro teams and stocking them with underpaid talents he later would bring to the majors.

It was Rickey who in essence invented baseball's minor-league system that still stands today.

Rickey also was known to squeeze every dollar out of every contract.

It was for these reasons that when Rickey signed Robinson, few observers believed Rickey's move had any higher calling other than to make a buck.

Most people remember Branch Rickey as a tough businessman and negotiator. This *Houston Chronicle* article discusses the Brooklyn Dodgers general manager and his social conscience.

Access this Web site from http://www.myreportlinks.com

to break baseball's color barrier and sign as many great African-American players as he could. In 1945, he had his eye on twenty-six-year-old Jackie Robinson.

Robinson was, quite simply, one of the greatest athletes anyone had seen. At UCLA, he ranked among the nation's best running backs in football and scorers in basketball. He also was a world-class long jumper, and he starred at shortstop for the Kansas City Monarchs of the Negro Leagues.

In 1945, Rickey met with Robinson, telling him of his plan to make him baseball's first black player of the twentieth century. Rickey was upfront, insisting Robinson would be abused by bigoted whites but that he had to absorb the punishment. Should Robinson ever retaliate, whites could use his "poor behavior" as an excuse to oust him from the league. "Mr. Rickey, do you want a ballplayer who's afraid to fight back?" Robinson asked. "I want a ballplayer with guts enough *not* to fight back," Rickey replied.[4]

Overcoming Resistance

Robinson understood his challenge, and on October 23, 1945, he signed with the Dodgers. Robinson played the 1946 season with Montreal, a minor-league team. Not surprisingly, he led the International League in batting average (.349) and sparked his club to the league championship.

Fans loved him, but that was in Canada. How would he fare in the more racially intolerant United States?

During spring training in 1947, Robinson played for Montreal. But Dodgers players knew that Rickey planned to promote Robinson to Brooklyn. Some members of the team put together a petition for Rickey, stating they opposed the idea of playing with an African American. Dodgers manager Leo Durocher called a team meeting and lambasted the insurgents. Rickey did the same.

Big Debut

On April 15, 1947, at Ebbets Field, Jackie Robinson made his major-league debut. No newsreel film exists of the event; the white-dominated media was not that interested. Only 26,623 fans attended the Opening Day game, most of whom were African American. Robinson, playing first base, went hitless, but he scored the winning run.

Robinson struggled early in the season, and he endured the abuse that Rickey predicted. Pitchers hit him with pitches nine times during the season, second most in the National League. Fielders hammered him with hard tags. Some opposing players and fans spewed verbal hatred. The Philadelphia Phillies were especially hostile, and death threats greeted Robinson in Cincinnati. But through it all, Robinson showed guts enough not to fight back.

⊖Changing People's Opinions

People were impressed by his class and courage, and Robinson won more and more supporters. During one game, Dodgers shortstop Pee Wee Reese threw his arm around his new pal for all to see. And in May, when St. Louis Cardinals players threatened to strike, National League President Ford Frick took a mighty stand.

"I do not care if half the league strikes," Frick exclaimed. "Those who do it will encounter quick retribution. They will be suspended, and I don't care if it wrecks the National League for five years. This is the United States of America, and one citizen has as much right to play as another."[5]

After several weeks of adjustment, Robinson developed into an offensive terror. A dynamic line-drive hitter, he also distracted pitchers with daring leadoffs at first base. The speedy, aggressive runner was a constant threat to steal second, third, and even home (a feat he pulled off twelve times during his first two seasons). Robinson finished the 1947 season with a .297 batting average. He led the league in stolen bases (29) and sacrifice bunts (28), and he ranked second with 125 runs scored. He not only won the MLB Rookie of the Year award, but he also finished fifth in voting for the NL's Most Valuable Player award.

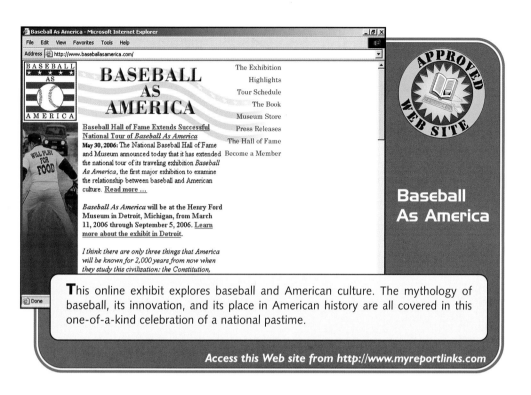

Baseball As America - Microsoft Internet Explorer

File   Edit   View   Favorites   Tools   Help

Address http://www.baseballasamerica.com/

BASEBALL AS AMERICA

Baseball Hall of Fame Extends Successful National Tour of *Baseball As America*
May 30, 2006: The National Baseball Hall of Fame and Museum announced today that it has extended the national tour of its traveling exhibition *Baseball As America*, the first major exhibition to examine the relationship between baseball and American culture. Read more ...

Baseball As America will be at the Henry Ford Museum in Detroit, Michigan, from March 11, 2006 through September 5, 2006. Learn more about the exhibit in Detroit.

I think there are only three things that America will be known for 2,000 years from now when they study this civilization: the Constitution,

The Exhibition
Highlights
Tour Schedule
The Book
Museum Store
Press Releases
The Hall of Fame
Become a Member

Baseball As America

This online exhibit explores baseball and American culture. The mythology of baseball, its innovation, and its place in American history are all covered in this one-of-a-kind celebration of a national pastime.

Access this Web site from http://www.myreportlinks.com

Near Misses

With Jackie Robinson wreaking havoc at the top of the order, the Dodgers drew a franchise-record 1,807,526 fans in 1947, leading the league in attendance. Brooklyn also won 94 games and the National League pennant. As in 1941, they geared up to play New York in the Subway Series.

Joe DiMaggio and the Yankees took the first two games of the World Series, but Brooklyn came back to win a 9–8 nail-biter. The Dodgers thought they had a chance to beat Yankees starter Bill Bevens in Game 4. Bevens could not find the plate in this contest, walking a World Series-record 10 batters. Yet the Dodgers could not hit him. With two outs in the bottom of the ninth, and the Yankees leading 2–1, Bevens was actually on the verge of a no-hitter. Fittingly, Bevens's two walks in the ninth doomed him. Cookie Lavagetto drove in both runners with a blast off the wall, sparking bedlam throughout Brooklyn.

The Yankees took Game 5, but the Dodgers won another classic in Game 6. In front of 74,065 fans, five-foot six-inch Dodgers outfielder Al Gionfriddo

▲ This team photo of the 1947 Brooklyn Dodgers shows the first racially integrated team in modern Major League Baseball history.

robbed DiMaggio of a home run, preserving a Brooklyn victory. Their jubilation, however, was short-lived, as the Yankees won the Series in seven games. After forty-five years of trying, Brooklyn still had not won a world title.

After a third-place finish in 1948, the Dodgers roared back to cop the NL flag in 1949. Robinson led the league in hitting (.342) and steals (37) while driving in 124 runs. In what would be the greatest season of his career, Robinson won the National League MVP award.

Clearly, Rickey's plan to win with African Americans was paying off. In 1949, two other dark-skinned Dodgers players—rookie pitcher Don Newcombe along with second-year catcher Roy Campanella—made the NL All-Star team. With a 97–57 record, Brooklyn earned another shot against the Yankees in the fall classic. The Yanks boasted an identical regular season record, but they frustrated the Dodgers repeatedly in the World Series. The Yankees won a 1–0, nail-biter in Game 1, and went on to win the Series in five games. But even that tough loss could not compare to the devastation of 1951.

Shot Down

In all of baseball history, no rivalry quite matched the Brooklyn Dodgers versus the New York Giants. The two clubs were the only big-league teams ever

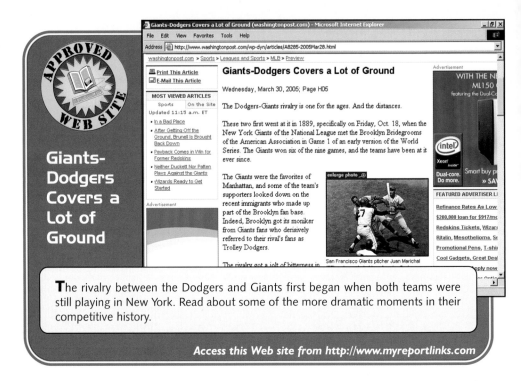

Giants-
Dodgers
Covers a
Lot of
Ground

Giants-Dodgers Covers a Lot of Ground

Wednesday, March 30, 2005; Page H05

The Dodgers-Giants rivalry is one for the ages. And the distances.

These two first went at it in 1889, specifically on Friday, Oct. 18, when the New York Giants of the National League met the Brooklyn Bridegrooms of the American Association in Game 1 of an early version of the World Series. The Giants won six of the nine games, and the teams have been at it ever since.

The Giants were the favorites of Manhattan, and some of the team's supporters looked down on the recent immigrants who made up part of the Brooklyn fan base. Indeed, Brooklyn got its moniker from Giants fans who derisively referred to their rival's fans as Trolley Dodgers.

The rivalry got a jolt of bitterness in

San Francisco Giants pitcher Juan Marichal

The rivalry between the Dodgers and Giants first began when both teams were still playing in New York. Read about some of the more dramatic moments in their competitive history.

Access this Web site from http://www.myreportlinks.com

to play in the same city, in the same league, at the same time. They played each other twenty-two times a year.

In 1951, Brooklyn fans did all the boasting. The Dodgers held a 13½-game lead in the National League as late as August 12. The Giants, though, refused to fold. Managed by former Dodgers skipper Leo Durocher and ignited by rookie Willie Mays, New York went 37–7 down the stretch to catch their hated rivals. A three-game playoff was scheduled to determine the NL champion, and the clubs split the first two contests.

Entering the bottom of the ninth during Game 3, the Dodgers led 4–1. The Giants, though, had one more comeback in them. Alvin Dark and Don Mueller singled, and with one out, Whitey Lockman doubled to make it 4–2. Dodgers pitcher Ralph Branca was called in to put out the fire.

With two men on, New York's Bobby Thomson stepped to the plate. On the second pitch, he drilled a shot that just cleared the left-field fence—and sent fans into hysterics. "The Giants win the pennant!" blared broadcaster Russ Hodges. "And they're going crazy! They're going crazy! Oh, ho!"[6] Thomson's homer was soon dubbed the "Shot Heard 'Round the World."

The Boys of Summer

After the war-ravaged 1940s, Americans welcomed the arrival of the 1950s. The Dodgers themselves took on a new look. In the broadcast booth in 1950, twenty-two-year-old Vin Scully—fresh out of Fordham University—teamed up with the esteemed Red Barber. After the season, Branch Rickey resigned and Walter O'Malley became the Dodgers' president and majority owner. A masterful businessman, O'Malley would blaze new trails for major-league baseball.

In 1952, the Dodgers won the pennant again. A strong, deep pitching staff and Gil Hodges's 32 homers propelled them to yet another Subway Series. This time, it looked like Dem Bums would finally prevail, as they won three of the first five

Duke Snider was the Dodgers center fielder for many years. A great player and fan favorite, he was elected to the National Baseball Hall of Fame in 1980.

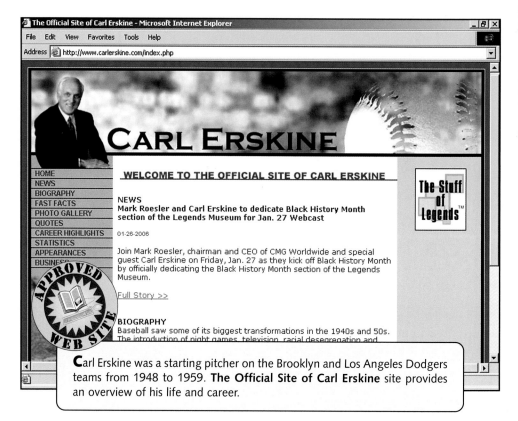

The Official Site of Carl Erskine - Microsoft Internet Explorer

File   Edit   View   Favorites   Tools   Help

Address http://www.carlerskine.com/index.php

CARL ERSKINE

HOME
NEWS
BIOGRAPHY
FAST FACTS
PHOTO GALLERY
QUOTES
CAREER HIGHLIGHTS
STATISTICS
APPEARANCES
BUSINESS

WELCOME TO THE OFFICIAL SITE OF CARL ERSKINE

The Stuff of Legends™

NEWS
Mark Roesler and Carl Erskine to dedicate Black History Month section of the Legends Museum for Jan. 27 Webcast

01-26-2006

Join Mark Roesler, chairman and CEO of CMG Worldwide and special guest Carl Erskine on Friday, Jan. 27 as they kick off Black History Month by officially dedicating the Black History Month section of the Legends Museum.

Full Story >>

BIOGRAPHY
Baseball saw some of its biggest transformations in the 1940s and 50s. The introduction of night games, television, racial desegregation and

Carl Erskine was a starting pitcher on the Brooklyn and Los Angeles Dodgers teams from 1948 to 1959. **The Official Site of Carl Erskine** site provides an overview of his life and career.

games. In the sixth inning of Game 6, Brooklyn's Duke Snider broke a scoreless tie with a home run. But the Yankees stormed back again, winning that game 3–2 and the next 4–2. "Wait till next year," continued as the Dodgers' halfhearted rallying cry.

In 1953, the Dodgers fielded their most glorious of teams. The subject of the classic Roger Kahn book *The Boys of Summer,* these Dodgers were beloved for their talent and charm. "The team wasn't made up of heroes on pedestals;" wrote Paul Adomites, "the players were guys who lived down the street and who got their hair cut by the same barber as your dad."[7]

A Dominant Team

Despite their humility, the 1953 Dodgers overpowered the competition. They scored more runs (955), hit more home runs (208), and won more games (105) than any Brooklyn team before or after. Carl Furillo ripped .344, Snider belted 42 home runs, and catcher Roy Campanella amassed 41 homers and 142 RBI. He won his second NL MVP award in three years. Historians rank this club's defense among the greatest in baseball history. Shortstop Pee Wee Reese and third baseman Billy Cox sealed tight the left side of the infield.

Yet incredibly enough, even this juggernaut could not beat the Yankees in the 1953 fall classic. Brooklyn batted .300 for the Series, but New York always seemed to get the big hit. The Yankees' Mickey Mantle belted a grand slam in Game 5, and feisty Billy Martin knocked in the Series-winning hit in the ninth inning of Game 6 at Yankee Stadium. The Yankees won their fifth consecutive World Series, a feat that has never been matched.

"Next Year" Arrives

In 1954, the reserved Walter Alston replaced Charlie Dressen as Dodgers manager. A year later, he led Brooklyn to the World Series against—who else?—the Yankees. By this point, the Dodgers-Yankees feud had reached the ferocity of Dodgers-Giants. "As a player, you couldn't help getting caught up in

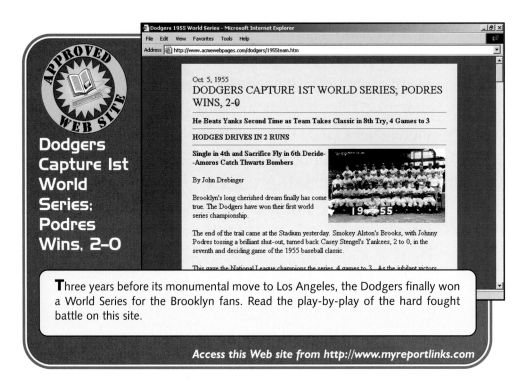

Dodgers
Capture 1st
World
Series;
Podres
Wins, 2–0

Dodgers 1955 World Series - Microsoft Internet Explorer

File   Edit   View   Favorites   Tools   Help

Address   http://www.acmewebpages.com/dodgers/1955team.htm

Oct. 5, 1955

DODGERS CAPTURE 1ST WORLD SERIES; PODRES WINS, 2–0

He Beats Yanks Second Time as Team Takes Classic in 8th Try, 4 Games to 3

HODGES DRIVES IN 2 RUNS

Single in 4th and Sacrifice Fly in 6th Decide--Amoros Catch Thwarts Bombers

By John Drebinger

Brooklyn's long cherished dream finally has come true. The Dodgers have won their first world series championship.

The end of the trail came at the Stadium yesterday. Smokey Alston's Brooks, with Johnny Podres tossing a brilliant shut-out, turned back Casey Stengel's Yankees, 2 to 0, in the seventh and deciding game of the 1955 baseball classic.

This gave the National League champions the series, 4 games to 3. As the jubilant victors

Three years before its monumental move to Los Angeles, the Dodgers finally won a World Series for the Brooklyn fans. Read the play-by-play of the hard fought battle on this site.

Access this Web site from http://www.myreportlinks.com

the rivalry," said Yankees pitcher Whitey Ford. "The enthusiasm was unbelievable. . . . We especially loved it because we usually beat [them] and we got great pleasure out of . . . shutting up their fans."[8]

Dodgers fans expected the worst. After all, they were 0–7 in fall classics, and 0–5 against the Yankees since 1941. Said Dodgers pitcher Carl Erskine, "You can't imagine the hunger that existed in my belly along with the rest of the guys to win a World Series."[9] In Game 1, both teams expressed their tenacity. Jackie Robinson stole home for Brooklyn. When Billy Martin tried to do the same for New York, catcher Roy Campanella swatted him with a brutal tag. Nevertheless, the Yankees won the first two games.

The Series moved to Ebbets Field for three straight games, and Brooklyn's sluggers came alive. Dem Bums prevailed 8–3, 8–5, and 5–3, with Duke Snider smashing 3 home runs. After Yankees ace Whitey Ford cruised in Game 6 (5–1), the stage was set for a Game 7 showdown.

The sixty-two thousand fans at Yankee Stadium expected their "Bronx Bombers" to tee off on young Dodgers pitcher Johnny Podres. But into the sixth inning, the crafty lefthander held a 2–0 lead. In the bottom of the sixth, with two Yankees on and none out, New York's Yogi Berra smashed what appeared to be a game-tying double to left

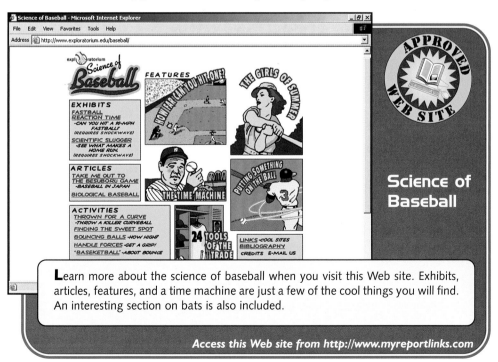

Learn more about the science of baseball when you visit this Web site. Exhibits, articles, features, and a time machine are just a few of the cool things you will find. An interesting section on bats is also included.

Access this Web site from http://www.myreportlinks.com

field. However, left fielder Sandy Amoros made a sensational running catch. He then wheeled and gunned down the runner retreating to first base for a spectacular double play.

⊜ Bums No More

Podres survived a scare in the eighth, but he set down the Yankees 1-2-3 in the ninth. When Elston Howard grounded out to shortstop at 3:43 P.M., concluding the 2–0 shutout, "next year" arrived. The Dodgers were world champions! Players ran to the mound and embraced their conquering pitcher.

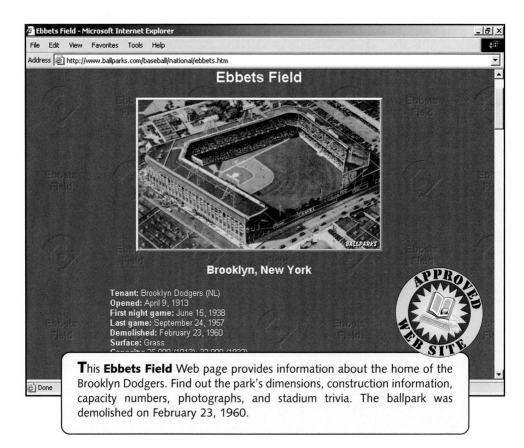

This **Ebbets Field** Web page provides information about the home of the Brooklyn Dodgers. Find out the park's dimensions, construction information, capacity numbers, photographs, and stadium trivia. The ballpark was demolished on February 23, 1960.

In the clubhouse, Erskine thought about gathering the guys for a prayer of thanksgiving. But it never happened. Players were too ecstatic, as was the entire borough of Brooklyn. "That night, nobody ate at home," remembered Dodgers fan Bill Reddy:

> People brought the food into the streets. There were dozens of block parties. They brought little electric stoves outside, cooking hamburgers in the streets. . . . And mind you, you could go to Williamsburg or to Garrison Beach or any other neighborhood in Brooklyn, and people were doing the same thing. People were marching across the Brooklyn Bridge in celebration. . . . We drove up McKeever Place, down Bedford Avenue, blowing our horns, throwing paper in the air. . . .[10]

The next day, the *New York Daily News* blared the headline: "Who's a Bum!" Not the Dodgers, fans responded. Not anymore.

So Long, Brooklyn

The Dodgers remained a power in 1956, thanks to 43 home runs by Duke Snider and an NL MVP season from Don Newcombe (27–7 record). They even won the first two games of the World Series against the Yankees. After that, however, the Brooklyn offense disappeared. After winning Games 3 and 4, New York took Game 5, 2–0, on Don Larsen's perfect game. Larsen retired all twenty-seven batters he faced en route to baseball immortality. The Dodgers eked out a 1–0 win in

Game 6, but they were crushed 9–0 in the Game 7 finale.

Brooklynites could deal with the Series loss, but far more troubling news emerged in 1956 and 1957: Owner Walter O'Malley wanted to move the team. A businessman first and foremost, O'Malley realized the shortcomings of Ebbets Field. Its seating capacity was only thirty-two thousand, and it was forty-three years old. The neighborhood was declining, as well-off residents were fleeing to the burgeoning suburbs. Attendance dropped, partly because fans could now watch games on their new television sets. At first, O'Malley thought about moving the team to another part of New York City. Then he pursued a more brazen plan.

⊜Taking the Team West

O'Malley liked the idea of relocating the Dodgers to Los Angeles. At the time, no major-league team had ever existed west of Kansas City because train travel to the West was too far. However, airplane travel gained popularity in the 1950s, and jet travel was about to emerge in the late 1950s. Eastern teams could fly to Los Angeles in just a few hours.

Meanwhile, Los Angeles was booming. In the 1950s, it joined New York, Chicago, and Philadelphia as the only American cities with populations exceeding 2 million. Since those cities supported at least two major-league teams, Los Angeles surely could maintain one big-league club. O'Malley dreamed of building a new ballpark in Los Angeles, with a huge parking lot. Baseball-starved fans would drive from all over Southern California to support the state's first major-league team. New York Giants owner Horace Stoneham had a similar idea, eyeing a move to San Francisco.

On May 29, 1957, the National League approved the relocation of both the Dodgers and Giants to California. O'Malley told fans that the approval only allowed him to explore possibilities. But savvy Brooklynites knew better. By the season finale, every fan at Ebbets Field knew they were watching "Brooklyn" play for the last time.

After the final out, fans roamed the field and ripped up clumps of turf as souvenirs. The organist played "Auld Lang Syne." For diehard Dodgers fans, the finality was gut-wrenching. Eight-year-old Charley Steiner called Walter O'Malley and bared his soul to his secretary. "I was crying and babbling like an idiot," said Steiner, a future ESPN broadcaster. "I said to her, 'How can you do this to me? This is my baseball team.'"[11] The secretary promised that Mr. O'Malley would get back to him. He never did.

Los Angeles Mayor Norris Poulson holds up a ceremonial plate that was given to him by Dodgers owner Walter O'Malley (right). The event pictured was a welcoming for the Dodgers' move to Los Angeles, held on April 18, 1958.

CALIFORNIA BOUND

On October 8, 1957, the Dodgers officially announced their move to Los Angeles. "It's the news I've been waiting for," said Los Angeles Mayor Norris Poulson. "It's wonderful. Now Los Angeles is major-league in every sense of the word."[1]

Dodgers owner Walter O'Malley would build his own playing field: a dream ballpark called Dodger Stadium. But the city of Los Angeles pitched in happily. The city council voted to cede three hundred acres of real estate for the new stadium. Known as Chavez Ravine, the hilly land was less than a ten-minute drive from downtown Los Angeles. The city also donated millions of dollars to clear the land and construct roads that led to the park.

For the first four seasons, the Dodgers had to squeeze a baseball diamond into a football stadium, the Los Angeles Memorial Coliseum. The outfield

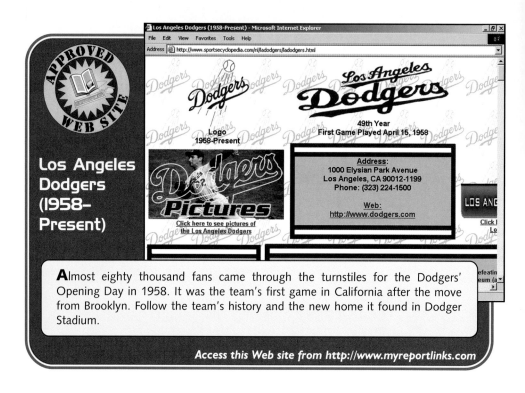

Los Angeles Dodgers (1958–Present)

Los Angeles Dodgers (1958-Present) - Microsoft Internet Explorer

File   Edit   View   Favorites   Tools   Help

Address   http://www.sportsecyclopedia.com/nl/ladodgers/ladodgers.html

Los Angeles Dodgers

Logo
1958-Present

49th Year
First Game Played April 15, 1958

Pictures

Click here to see pictures of
the Los Angeles Dodgers

Address:
1000 Elysian Park Avenue
Los Angeles, CA 90012-1199
Phone: (323) 224-1500

Web:
http://www.dodgers.com

Almost eighty thousand fans came through the turnstiles for the Dodgers' Opening Day in 1958. It was the team's first game in California after the move from Brooklyn. Follow the team's history and the new home it found in Dodger Stadium.

Access this Web site from http://www.myreportlinks.com

dimensions were ridiculous. The right-center-field fence was a whopping 380 feet away. To compensate for the extremely short distance down the left-field line (251 feet), the Dodgers constructed a 42-foot screen to prevent home runs.

On Opening Day in 1958, 78,672 fans packed the Coliseum to watch the Dodgers face their old rival: the Giants, who now played in San Francisco. The Dodgers broke their team attendance record in 1958, drawing 1,845,556 fans. However, the team finished with a 71–83 record. The tragic loss of superstar catcher Roy Campanella was largely to blame. The previous winter, Campanella was permanently paralyzed in an auto accident. On May 7, 1959, 93,103 fans filled the Coliseum for "Roy Campanella Night," an exhibition game between the Dodgers and the Yankees. It was, and remains, the largest crowd ever to watch a major-league baseball game.

Sherry and the Psychic

In spring training 1959, *Parade* magazine asked psychic Peter Hurkos to examine the National League teams and predict who would win the pennant. Hurkos knew little about baseball (he was from the Netherlands), but he felt strongly that the Dodgers would prevail. *Parade* readers laughed. How could a seventh-place team from 1958 win the 1959 NL title?

Manager Walter Alston's team was not that talented, but no club played with greater desire. Surprisingly, a rookie pitcher proved to be the Dodgers' secret weapon. Promoted from the minors during the season, Larry Sherry won his last seven decisions. He helped Los Angeles finish the season tied for first place.

In a best-of-three playoff versus the Milwaukee Braves, the Dodgers won Game 1 thanks to seven-plus scoreless innings of relief by Sherry. Eerily, the scout who had signed Sherry, Red Corriden, died of a heart attack while watching him pitch in this game. The Dodgers then won Game 2 to clinch the pennant, making the psychic's "crazy" prediction come true.

Los Angeles faced the Chicago White Sox in the World Series. The speedy "Go Go" Sox won the opener 11–0, but then they ran out of steam. Sherry pitched magnificently in relief in Games 2, 3, 4, and 6. The Dodgers won every one of those games to clinch their first world title on the West Coast. No one had predicted *that*—not even Peter Hurkos.

Almost Magical

In 1962, fans flocked to the brand-new Dodger Stadium, the most exciting destination in California since Disneyland. Mayor Poulson had correctly predicted that the Dodgers would break the major-league attendance record that year. As it turned out, the 2,755,184 fans who spun through the turnstiles had plenty to cheer about. Maury Wills became the first big-leaguer in modern history to steal 100 bases in a season. The massive Frank Howard (six feet seven inches, 255 pounds) clobbered 31 home runs. Tommy Davis amassed 153 RBI. And fireballing lefty Sandy Koufax threw a no-hitter in one game and struck out eighteen batters in another.

Adding to the excitement, both the Dodgers and their rival Giants tied for first with 101–61 records. In their best-of-three playoff, Los Angeles lost the opener 8–0, but won an 8–7 thriller in he bottom of the ninth of Game 2. In Game 3, the Giants worked their Bobby Thomson-like magic all over again. Trailing 4–2 in the top of the ninth, the Giants rallied for 4 runs. The last two came on a bases loaded walk and an infield error, and San Francisco won 6–4. What could have been the most magical of seasons ended in bitter frustration.

Sandy's Golden Touch

In 1963, some of the Dodgers lost their luster. Maury Wills stole 64 fewer bases, and Tommy Davis drove in only 88 runs. Nevertheless, Los Angeles repeated as the NL champion thanks to the extraordinary heroics of one man: Sandy Koufax.

Born and raised in Brooklyn, Koufax debuted with the Dodgers at age nineteen in 1955. The lefty boasted an explosive fastball and a wicked curveball, and by 1962 he began to throw with surgeon-like precision. In 1963, he blew away National League hitters. He posted the best record in the league (25–5) while leading the NL in ERA (1.88) and strikeouts (306). Koufax no-hit the Giants on May 11, and he ran away with the NL MVP award.

With Koufax and the intimidating Don Drysdale (19 wins), the Dodgers could outpitch anyone. They proved it in the 1963 World Series against the Yankees. Los Angeles won the opener

The 1962 Dodgers boasted an excellent pitching staff. From left to right are Don Drysdale, Pete Richert, Stan Williams, Sandy Koufax, and Johnny Podres.

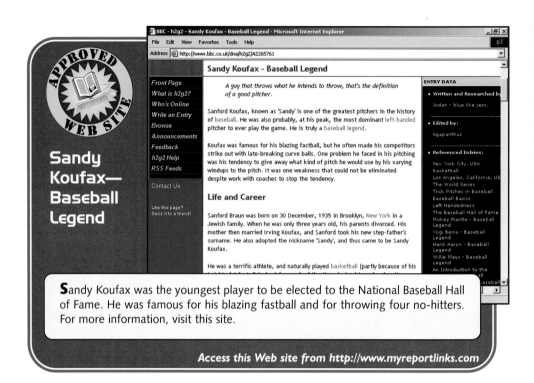

Sandy Koufax—Baseball Legend

Sandy Koufax was the youngest player to be elected to the National Baseball Hall of Fame. He was famous for his blazing fastball and for throwing four no-hitters. For more information, visit this site.

Access this Web site from http://www.myreportlinks.com

5–2, as Koufax set a World Series record with 15 strikeouts. The next day, Johnny Podres—the "Yankee killer" from 1955—prevailed 4–1. In a brilliant pitcher's duel in Game 3, Drysdale outshone Jim Bouton 1–0.

Yankees ace Whitey Ford took the hill in Game 4, but not even the winningest pitcher in World Series history could match up against Koufax. Aided by a 450-foot home run by big Frank Howard, Koufax triumphed 2–1. The Yankees had not only suffered a rare World Series defeat, but they also were swept for the first time ever. New York superstar Mickey Mantle tipped his cap to the

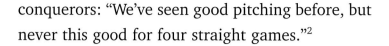

conquerors: "We've seen good pitching before, but never this good for four straight games."[2]

Down and Back Up

In 1964, the Dodgers nose-dived to a tie for sixth place with an 80–82 record. Their brilliant pitching could not offset their feeble offensive attack (614 runs scored). In 1965, Los Angeles scored even fewer runs (608), but their pitching was so sensational that they made a run for the NL pennant. A game on September 9 proved to be a metaphor for their season. The Dodgers mustered just one hit in nine innings against Bob Hendley of the Chicago Cubs. But Koufax threw a perfect game, retiring all twenty-seven batters he faced. Drysdale would finish the season at 23–12, while Koufax would go 26–8 with 382 strikeouts—a new major-league record.

In the latter weeks of the 1965 season, the Dodgers and Giants battled ferociously for first place. A brawl between the two teams on August 22 ignited their passions. By late September, the Giants had won nineteen of their last twenty games while Los Angeles was in the midst of a 15–1 streak. Koufax proved to be the difference. After firing back-to-back shutouts, he beat Milwaukee 2–1 on October 2 to clinch the NL title.

The Dodgers lost the first two games of the 1965 World Series to heavy-hitting Minnesota.

The Twins, however, felt uncomfortable in Los Angeles' spacious "pitcher's park." The Dodgers won Games 3, 4, and 5 at home, allowing just two runs over the three Games. A Twins win in Game 6 set up a winner-take-all matchup in Game 7.

It was Drysdale's turn to pitch, but manager Walter Alston thought about starting Koufax—who had tossed a shutout three days earlier. Drysdale proved to be a good sport. "Skipper," he told Alston, "whatever you decide is fine with me."[3] The manager went with Koufax, and the Twins could not touch him. Koufax pitched a three-hit shutout, making Alston the first National League manager ever to win four world titles.

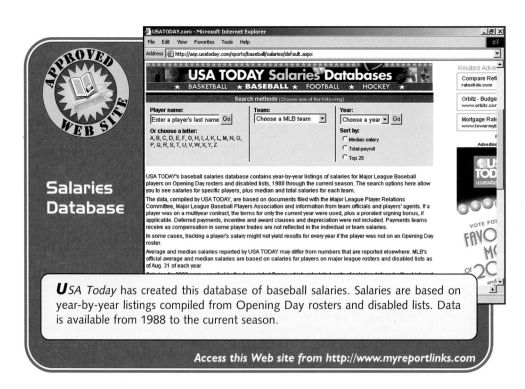

USA Today has created this database of baseball salaries. Salaries are based on year-by-year listings compiled from Opening Day rosters and disabled lists. Data is available from 1988 to the current season.

Access this Web site from http://www.myreportlinks.com

In 1966, Koufax and Drysdale missed all of spring training in contract disputes. Everyone knew that without their superstar pitchers, the team was in big trouble. Eventually, Koufax signed for a $120,000 salary and Drysdale $105,000. Again, pitching carried the team. The Dodgers' 2.62 earned run average was the lowest in the major leagues since 1943. Koufax went 27–9 and led the NL in ERA (1.73) for the fifth straight season. Closer Phil Regan was equally amazing. "The Vulture" went 14–1 with 21 saves and a 1.62 ERA.

The End of an Era

Again, the Dodgers and Giants battled to the wire in 1966. And once again, Koufax came to the rescue, clinching the pennant in the season finale. Fans expected sensational pitching in the World Series, and they got it—from the Baltimore Orioles. The Dodgers scored 2 runs in the first three innings of Game 1, and then did not score again for the entire Series! Jim Palmer, Wally Bunker, and Dave McNally shut out Los Angeles in Games 2, 3, and 4, completing the sweep.

After the World Series, Koufax announced his retirement at age thirty. His left elbow was so damaged that further pitching could have left him permanently disabled. With Koufax gone, and the lineup void of sluggers, Los Angeles was doomed. The Dodgers finished in eighth place in 1967 and seventh in 1968, and they failed to challenge for the pennant through 1970. In the early 1970s, however, a new crop of ballplayers would energize Dodger Stadium.

Bleeding Dodger Blue

The Dodgers-Giants rivalry, arguably the greatest in baseball history, continued to rage in 1971. San Francisco won 90 games, one more than Los Angeles, to capture the NL West Division title. In 1973, Los Angeles began to reload with a new, exciting cast of characters. In June of that year, the Dodgers fielded Steve Garvey at first base, Davey Lopes at second, Bill Russell at shortstop, and Ron Cey at third. This quartet would play as a unit for eight-and-a-half years, setting a record for longevity for a major-league infield.

All four of these players were National League All-Stars at one time or another. The clean-cut Garvey smashed line drives and homers with his Popeye-like forearms. Lopes, known for his furry mustache, stole bases at will. Russell kept the offense clicking with bunts, steals, and timely hits. And Cey, nicknamed "The Penguin" because he ran like one, socked scores of home runs.

In 1974, this infield saw plenty of Dodgers relief pitcher Mike Marshall. The "rubber-armed" hurler appeared in 106 games, a major-league record that still stands. The 1974 Dodgers beat

Pittsburgh in the National League Championship Series. However, they were no match for the mighty Oakland A's, who won the World Series in five games.

In 1975 and 1976, the Dodgers finished second in the West Division behind the powerful Cincinnati Reds—the "Big Red Machine." But after Walter Alston retired, new manager Tommy Lasorda instilled new life into the ballclub. "I bleed Dodger blue!" beamed the team's manager and No. 1 fan.[4] In 1977, Lasorda rode the fortunes of pitcher Don Sutton (the All-Star Game MVP) and a quartet of power hitters. Garvey, Cey, and outfielders Reggie Smith and Dusty Baker became

This project by the Society for American Baseball Research (SABR) produces comprehensive biographies of major-league players, managers, and owners. Search or browse for your favorites.

Access this Web site from http://www.myreportlinks.com

the first big-leaguers to belt 30 home runs apiece for the same team. The Dodgers beat Philadelphia in the NLCS but lost to the Yankees in the World Series. Reggie Jackson's 3 home runs in Game 6 were the killer blows.

California Phenomenon

In 1978, Los Angeles became the first team ever to surpass 3 million in attendance. Everyone, it seemed, loved the Dodgers, who symbolized the good cheer of sunny California. Lasorda's boys again defeated the Phillies in the NLCS, then once again fell to New York in the fall classic. Los Angeles rookie Bob Welch struck out Jackson

APPROVED WEB SITE

An In-Depth Look at Dodger Stadium's Effects

The Hardball Times

| Home | Articles | Extras | Teams | Stats |

October 9, 2006

Lineup
Brian Borawski
John Brattain
Craig Burley
Chris Constancio
David Gassko
Aaron Gleeman
Ben Jacobs
Jeff Sackmann
Dave Studeman
Steve Treder
Bryan Tsao
John Walsh

An In-Depth Look at Dodger Stadium's Effects
by Tom Meagher
February 17, 2005

Print this Article
E-mail this Article

Each ballpark has different effects on each player. Since each team is composed of different players and since a team can choose players who will benefit from playing in the ballpark the team calls home, there is an innate potential of selection bias in park factors. Furthermore, the effects a ballpark has are interrelated. A long fly ball can be a home run in one park and an out in another; a long fly ball hit with less hang time could be a home run in the first park and a double in the second.

On top of that, even 81 full games of data are far from an optimal sample size. 243 full games of data is a sub-optimal sample size. In addition, new parks are often introduced into the league and different teams visit different parks with differing frequencies and at different times season to season, which is of significance since weather plays a substantial role in how many runs are

Every ballpark has its good points, as well as its bad ones. For instance, Dodger Stadium is said to be tough on ground-ball pitchers and perhaps a better park for pitchers who cause batters to hit fly balls. Learn more about the science of stadium design when you visit this site.

Access this Web site from http://www.myreportlinks.com

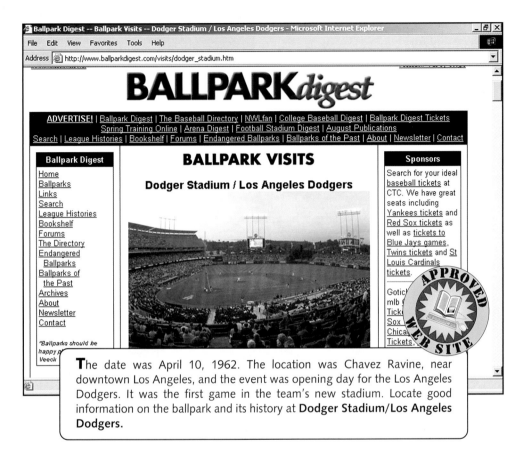

Ballpark Digest -- Ballpark Visits -- Dodger Stadium / Los Angeles Dodgers - Microsoft Internet Explorer

File   Edit   View   Favorites   Tools   Help

Address http://www.ballparkdigest.com/visits/dodger_stadium.htm

BALLPARK*digest*

ADVERTISE! | Ballpark Digest | The Baseball Directory | NWLfan | College Baseball Digest | Ballpark Digest Tickets
Spring Training Online | Arena Digest | Football Stadium Digest | August Publications
Search | League Histories | Bookshelf | Forums | Endangered Ballparks | Ballparks of the Past | About | Newsletter | Contact

Ballpark Digest

Home
Ballparks
Links
Search
League Histories
Bookshelf
Forums
The Directory
Endangered
 Ballparks
Ballparks of
 the Past
Archives
About
Newsletter
Contact

"Ballparks should be
happy p
Veeck

BALLPARK VISITS

Dodger Stadium / Los Angeles Dodgers

Sponsors

Search for your ideal
baseball tickets at
CTC. We have great
seats including
Yankees tickets and
Red Sox tickets as
well as tickets to
Blue Jays games,
Twins tickets and St
Louis Cardinals
tickets.

Gotic
mlb
Tick
Sox
Chica
Tickets

APPROVED WEB SITE

The date was April 10, 1962. The location was Chavez Ravine, near downtown Los Angeles, and the event was opening day for the Los Angeles Dodgers. It was the first game in the team's new stadium. Locate good information on the ballpark and its history at **Dodger Stadium/Los Angeles Dodgers**.

to end Game 1, but the Yankees prevailed in six games.

Were the Dodgers doomed against the Yankees—just like they were in the 1940s and 1950s? In 1981, Los Angeles would get one more crack at their longtime rival. And this time, they would not be denied.

The baseball world was taken by storm by rookie pitcher Fernando Valenzuela during the 1981 season. That year, the Dodgers won the World Series by beating the New York Yankees.

MANIA AND MIRACLES 4

Though largely forgotten by historians, the last weekend of the 1980 season remains bittersweet to Dodgers fans. Los Angeles entered the last three games trailing the Houston Astros by three games in the NL West. The two teams met for a series at Dodger Stadium. Each game was decided by one run, and the Dodgers won them all: 3–2, 2–1, and 4–3. In a one-game playoff, however, Houston prevailed 7–1.

The following spring, all of America got caught up in "Fernandomania." Fernando Valenzuela, a portly, affable rookie from Mexico, baffled hitters with his left-handed screwball. Through May 8, he was 7–0 with five shutouts and the lowest ERA anyone had ever seen: 0.29! Lasorda could not stop raving about his pitching sensation. "Why does everyone love him?" Lasorda asked rhetorically. "Maybe they see him like a teddy bear and

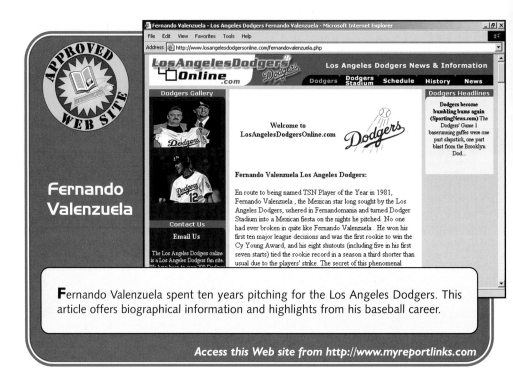

Fernando Valenzuela spent ten years pitching for the Los Angeles Dodgers. This article offers biographical information and highlights from his baseball career.

Access this Web site from http://www.myreportlinks.com

want to hold him, or like a little baby with big cheeks that they want to hug."[1]

Valenzuela eventually cooled off, and on June 12, big-league baseball stopped completely. A two-month strike by major-league players deprived Americans of the national pastime for much of the summer. Play resumed in August, and the Dodgers made the playoffs thanks to a dominant pitching staff. Due to the strike, four teams in each league made the playoffs. Los Angeles defeated both Houston and the Montreal Expos three games to two. Game 5 of the NLCS would forever be known as "Blue Monday": Los Angeles' Rick Monday won the game 2–1 with a homer in the top of the ninth.

In the World Series, the Yankees seemed destined to bury the Dodgers again, winning the first two games at home. But Los Angeles came storming back at Dodger Stadium. Valenzuela won Game 3, 5–4, and the Dodgers survived an 8–7 donnybrook in Game 4. Los Angeles took the next game 2–1, thanks to back-to-back homers in the seventh inning by slugger Pedro Guerrero and catcher Steve Yeager. In Game 6 at Yankee Stadium, the Dodgers poured it on in the middle innings and routed New York 9–2. Upon the final out, Lasorda practically flew out of the dugout, arms flailing, roaring in delight. The Dodgers' top cheerleader had finally won his first world championship.

The Miracles of '88

In February 1982, the Dodgers traded second baseman Davey Lopes, breaking up the longest-playing infield in history. Soon afterward, Steve Garvey and Ron Cey also left Los Angeles. Nevertheless, strong pitching kept the Dodgers competitive throughout the 1980s. They won the division in 1983 before losing in the playoffs to Philadelphia. Los Angeles took the NL West in 1985 thanks to the heroics of pitcher Orel Hershiser (19–3). Again they lost the NLCS, falling to St. Louis.

On September 16, 1987, Pope John Paul II celebrated Mass at Dodger Stadium. Perhaps his visit sparked the Dodger "miracles" of 1988. More

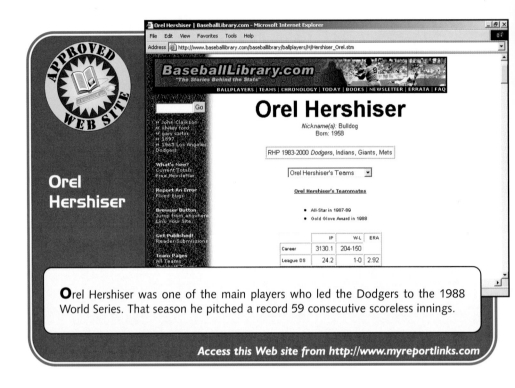

Orel Hershiser was one of the main players who led the Dodgers to the 1988 World Series. That season he pitched a record 59 consecutive scoreless innings.

Access this Web site from http://www.myreportlinks.com

likely, it was the tenacity of two special players: "Bulldog" Hershiser and outfielder Kirk Gibson.

With the Detroit Tigers, Gibson blasted rooftop homers and ran like a locomotive. He signed with the Dodgers in 1988 and immediately impressed his teammates with his fierce intensity. He was named the year's NL MVP. Hershiser, meanwhile, pitched shutout after shutout down the stretch. He ended the season with a major-league record 59 consecutive scoreless innings. Their efforts led to the division title followed by a series triumph over the New York Mets in the NLCS. Gibson belted 2 homers in the series, and Hershiser tossed a shutout in Game 7.

The Oakland A's were heavy favorites in the 1988 World Series. However, after Gibson's epic homer in Game 1 (see Chapter 1), the Athletics never recovered. Hershiser not only authored another shutout in Game 2, but he also cracked a single and two doubles! In the Game 5 finale, Hershiser was so excited that he sang hymns to himself to calm down. It worked, as he allowed just four hits over nine innings in a 5–2 Dodgers victory.

In his last 101 $\frac{2}{3}$ innings of pitching in 1988, Hershiser tossed scoreless ball in 96 of them. "I don't know if we will ever again see the likes of what [Orel has] done," Gibson said. "He'll go down in history."[2]

No Titles, Lots of Highlights

From the 1940s through the 1980s, the Dodgers made the World Series at least twice per decade. But from 1989 through 2005, they did not make the fall classic even once. In fact, they did not even reach the NL Championship Series. Sure, they came close on several occasions. In 1991, they finished in second place by one game behind Atlanta. Los Angeles was in a tie for first place when the 1994 season was ended by a strike. The Dodgers made the playoffs in 1995, but they were swept by Cincinnati in the NL Division Series. A year later, Atlanta swept Los Angeles in the NLDS.

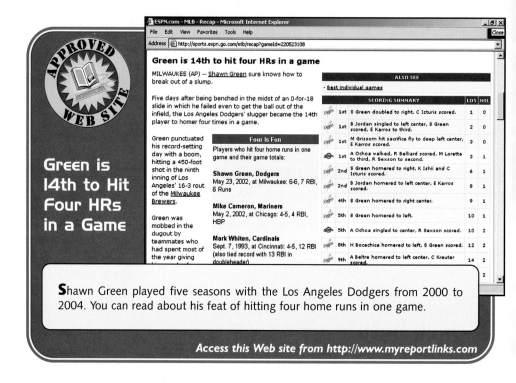

Green is 14th to Hit Four HRs in a Game

ESPN.com - MLB - Recap - Microsoft Internet Explorer

File   Edit   View   Favorites   Tools   Help   Close

Address   http://sports.espn.go.com/mlb/recap?gameId=220523108

Green is 14th to hit four HRs in a game

MILWAUKEE (AP) -- Shawn Green sure knows how to break out of a slump.

Five days after being benched in the midst of an 0-for-18 slide in which he failed even to get the ball out of the infield, the Los Angeles Dodgers' slugger became the 14th player to homer four times in a game.

Green punctuated his record-setting day with a boom, hitting a 450-foot shot in the ninth inning of Los Angeles' 16-3 rout of the Milwaukee Brewers.

Green was mobbed in the dugout by teammates who had spent most of the year giving

			ALSO SEE
			· Best individual games

Four Is Fun

Players who hit four home runs in one game and their game totals:

Shawn Green, Dodgers
May 23, 2002, at Milwaukee: 6-6, 7 RBI, 6 Runs

Mike Cameron, Mariners
May 2, 2002, at Chicago: 4-5, 4 RBI, HBP

Mark Whiten, Cardinals
Sept. 7, 1993, at Cincinnati: 4-5, 12 RBI (also tied record with 13 RBI in doubleheader)

SCORING SUMMARY		LOS	MIL
1st	S Green doubled to right, C Izturis scored.	1	0
1st	B Jordan singled to left center, S Green scored, E Karros to third.	2	0
1st	M Grissom hit sacrifice fly to deep left center, E Karros scored.	3	0
1st	A Ochoa walked, R Belliard scored, M Loretta to third, R Sexson to second.	3	1
2nd	S Green homered to right, K Ishii and C Izturis scored.	6	1
2nd	B Jordan homered to left center, E Karros scored.	8	1
4th	S Green homered to right center.	9	1
5th	S Green homered to left.	10	1
5th	A Ochoa singled to center, R Sexson scored.	10	2
8th	H Bocachica homered to left, S Green scored.	12	2
9th	A Beltre homered to left center, C Kreuter scored.	14	2
			2

Shawn Green played five seasons with the Los Angeles Dodgers from 2000 to 2004. You can read about his feat of hitting four home runs in one game.

Access this Web site from http://www.myreportlinks.com

And in 2004, they lost to St. Louis three games to one in the Division Series.

Despite the frustrations, the Dodgers provided enough thrills to pack the park on a regular basis. In the 1990s, the organization produced one young star after another. In fact, beginning in 1992, five straight Dodgers won the NL Rookie of the Year award: Eric Karros, Mike Piazza, Raul Mondesi, Hideo Nomo, and Todd Hollandsworth.

Piazza quickly emerged as a superstar catcher. He averaged .337 with 33 homers in his five full seasons with the Dodgers. Karros smashed 270 homers for Los Angeles, setting a Los Angeles Dodgers record. Mondesi became the first Dodger

Star relief pitcher Eric Gagne won the 2003 National League Cy Young Award as a member of the Los Angeles Dodgers.

to belt 30 homers and steal 30 bases in the same season (1997 and again in 1999).

Nomo, meanwhile, became an international sensation in 1995. As the first Japanese-born player in the majors in thirty years, he inspired California's large Asian population. His twisting, explosive delivery resembled a tornado, and he "blew away" NL hitters. Nomo started the All-Star Game as a rookie, and he led the NL in strikeouts with 236. A year earlier, Dodgers pitcher Chan Ho Park became the first Korean-born player in the big leagues.

In 2001, lanky outfielder Shawn Green set a Dodgers record by socking 49 home runs. A year later, he cracked 42—including 4 in one game on May 23. Green also laced a single and a double that day, giving him a major-league record 19 total bases for the game. Green's performance was so exceptional that the crowd gave him a standing ovation—and he was playing in Milwaukee!

⊜They Love Their Dodgers

From 2002 to 2004, Eric Gagne reigned as a dominant closer, averaging over 50 saves per year. Over one long stretch, he set a big-league record by converting 84 save opportunities in a row. In 2004, third baseman Adrian Beltre walloped 48 home runs to lead the league. He and Gagne helped keep the turnstiles spinning.

Even in 2005, when the Dodgers won just 71 games, the team drew 3 million fans for the tenth consecutive season. The team attendance of 3,603,646 led the league, and it was their highest total since 1982. It proved conclusively that, win or lose, Southern Californians love their Dodgers.

In 2006, new manager Grady Little piloted an exciting Dodgers team. Nomar Garciaparra, a former All-Star shortstop in the American League, moved to first base and powered the offense. On May 19, the Dodgers cracked 25 hits in one game to set a franchise record. In August, they won eleven straight games. But these feats were nothing compared to the fireworks on September 18.

Entering the game, Los Angeles was in a dogfight with San Diego for first place in the NL West. Going into the bottom of the ninth, the Padres led by four runs. Unbelievably, Jeff Kent, J. D. Drew, Russell Martin, and Marlon Anderson belted consecutive home runs, tying the score! After San Diego moved ahead 10–9 in the 10th, Garciaparra won it with a two-run homer in the bottom of the inning.

The Dodgers made the playoffs as a wildcard, and they were swept by the Mets in the opening round. However, their September 18 miracle was one their fans would never forget.

Red Barber announced Dodgers games from 1939 to 1953. He was one of the most highly respected broadcasters in the United States.

THE MASTERMINDS 5

The Dodgers have a reputation as a classy organization. However, a wide range of characters have run the ballclub, including a war hero, a gambler, a cheapskate, and a hugger. Discussed below are the most influential executives, managers, and broadcasters in Dodgers history.

Larry MacPhail

Considering his military career, it is not surprising that Larry MacPhail took chances as a baseball executive. As an Army captain during World War I, he had contributed to a plot to kidnap German leader Kaiser Wilhelm. As a lieutenant colonel in WWII, he assisted America's secretary of war.

MacPhail first made his mark on baseball in 1935. Working for the Cincinnati Reds, he orchestrated the first night game in major-league history,

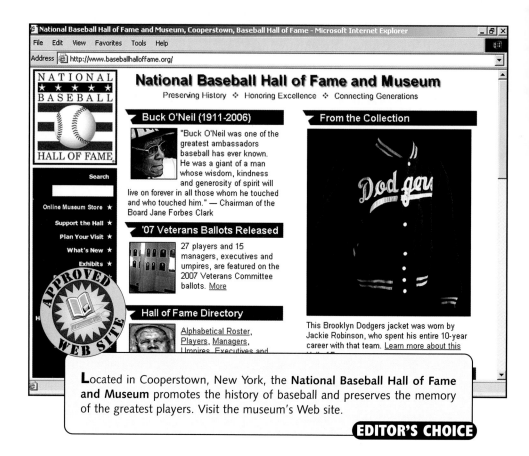

Located in Cooperstown, New York, the **National Baseball Hall of Fame and Museum** promotes the history of baseball and preserves the memory of the greatest players. Visit the museum's Web site.

EDITOR'S CHOICE

on May 24. After becoming the Dodgers' general manager in 1938, he helped usher in the era of broadcasting baseball games over the radio. His innovations with the Dodgers included a yellow baseball during spring training and the hiring of Babe Ruth as a Dodgers coach.

As GM, MacPhail acquired such stars as Pee Wee Reese, Joe Medwick, and Billy Herman. He had a love-hate relationship with hotheaded manager Leo Durocher. He fired him many times, only to rehire him the following morning. In 1941, MacPhail and Durocher's Dodgers won their first pennant in twenty-one years.

After World War II, MacPhail led the New York Yankees to greatness. He also helped introduce air travel to baseball. MacPhail and his son, baseball executive Lee MacPhail, are the only father and son in the Baseball Hall of Fame.

Leo Durocher

Leo Durocher was no choirboy. He hung out at the racetrack and associated with gangsters. On the field, "Leo the Lip" argued nose to nose with umpires until he inevitably was tossed out of the games. But Durocher did not believe that good behavior equaled success. As he famously said, "Nice guys finish last."[1]

What Durocher had was a brilliant baseball mind and a passion for success. In his first eight years as Brooklyn's manager (1939 to 1946), he finished with a winning record seven times. In 1941 he led the Dodgers to the World Series for the first time in twenty-one years. He showed some class in the spring of 1947, when he offered his full support of Jackie Robinson. "I don't care if the guy is yellow or black . . .," he said. "I'm the manager of this team and I say he plays."[2]

Ironically, Durocher missed all of 1947 himself, as he was suspended for gambling. A year later, he signed on to skipper the crosstown rival New York Giants. All told, Durocher managed twenty-four years in the major leagues and became the fifth manager ever to win two thousand games. He is enshrined in the Baseball Hall of Fame.

Red Barber

In the hustle and bustle of Brooklyn, ball fans found southern comfort on the radio. From 1939 to 1953, the folksy, friendly Red Barber broadcast Brooklyn Dodgers games. While committed to objective reporting (he avoided asserting his opinions), Barber wove in charming catchphrases. New Yorkers grinned big when he exclaimed one of his amusing phrases, such as "running like a bunny with his tail on fire!"[3]

For the Cincinnati Reds on Opening Day in 1934, Barber announced the first major-league game he ever saw. From there, he continued as a broadcasting pioneer. On May 24, 1935, in Cincinnati, he called the majors' first night game. On August 26, 1939, he was behind the mike for Major League Baseball's first televised contest.

Over the years, Barber worked in the booth with Vin Scully, Ernie Harwell, and Mel Allen. Each became award-winning play-by-play men—largely because of Barber. "Probably more than any announcer, we learned from him," said Harwell, "every one of us."[4]

⊖ Branch Rickey

When Branch Rickey became general manager of the Dodgers in 1942, he had already made his mark on the game. With the St. Louis Cardinals, he had established the first farm system—a collection of minor-league teams controlled by the major-league club. In Brooklyn, Rickey continued as a prolific innovator.

In Vero Beach, Florida, Rickey established baseball's first full-time spring training facility. Eventually, every big-league team would have its own preseason home, in either Florida or Arizona. Rickey also encouraged the use of batting helmets, batting cages, and pitching machines. Of course, his greatest gift to the game was breaking Major League Baseball's color barrier.

Ever since he coached at Ohio-Wesleyan in the early 1900s, Rickey had been sympathetic to the plight of African Americans. On a road trip to South Bend, Indiana, Ohio-Wesleyan player Charles Thomas was denied a room to a hotel because he was black. Rickey convinced management to let Thomas share a room with him. The player, though, was humiliated. "Black skin, black skin," Thomas said, rubbing his arms and crying. "If only I could make it white."[5]

Thus, Rickey felt great satisfaction in signing Jackie Robinson on October 23, 1945. The savvy GM soon acquired other outstanding African-American players, including catcher Roy Campanella and pitcher Don Newcombe. Rickey left the team in 1950, but the talent he had acquired led to great success. From 1952 to 1956, the Dodgers won the NL pennant four times.

▲ Branch Rickey was the beloved team president and part owner of the Brooklyn Dodgers. Here, he is having a chat with three Dodgers players. Jackie Robinson is to the right, Gene Hermanski is to the immediate left, and Gil Hodges is to the far left.

⊖Walter O'Malley

When Dodgers owner Walter O'Malley moved the team to Los Angeles, he endured the wrath of Brooklynites. Yet Los Angeles fans had their own beefs with him. In order to get fans to come to Dodger Stadium, O'Malley refused to show home games on television. Moreover, those who arrived at the ballpark on warm days were faced with an infuriating dilemma: buy overpriced drinks or go thirsty. O'Malley had deliberately built the stadium without drinking fountains!

That said, no one could deny O'Malley's vision and brilliance. After earning degrees in engineering and law, O'Malley became a hugely successful

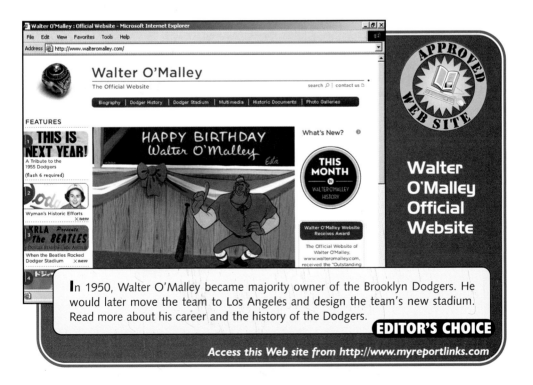

In 1950, Walter O'Malley became majority owner of the Brooklyn Dodgers. He would later move the team to Los Angeles and design the team's new stadium. Read more about his career and the history of the Dodgers.

EDITOR'S CHOICE

Access this Web site from http://www.myreportlinks.com

Walter Alston appears confident and relaxed as he talks to reporters after a game during the 1956 World Series. A very successful manager, Alston is a Dodgers legend.

lawyer and businessman. He became part-owner of the Brooklyn Dodgers in 1945 and eventually took controlling interest of the team.

By the mid-1950s, O'Malley realized he could make more money if he moved the Dodgers. He believed that Los Angeles, with its booming population, was an untapped gold mine for baseball. O'Malley used his own money to build Dodger Stadium, and fans flocked to the ballpark in record numbers.

Through the 1970s, O'Malley reigned as baseball's most powerful owner, with strong influence over MLB Commissioner Bowie Kuhn. After O'Malley died in 1979, his son, Peter O'Malley, took over the team for the next eighteen years.

Walter Alston

The son of a poor sharecropper, Walter Alston struck out in his one and only major-league at bat, in 1936. Yet two decades later, he came back to conquer the baseball world.

Beginning in 1940, Alston began managing in the minor leagues. He was quiet, conservative, and stoic, but he commanded his players' attention with his physical strength and chair-throwing temper. In 1954, the Dodgers gave him a chance to manage the big-league club.

One year later, Alston led the power-hitting Dodgers to the world championship—Brooklyn's first. When his team moved to Dodger Stadium,

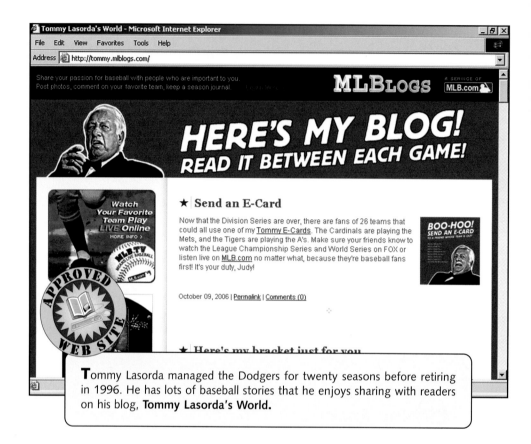

Tommy Lasorda managed the Dodgers for twenty seasons before retiring in 1996. He has lots of baseball stories that he enjoys sharing with readers on his blog, **Tommy Lasorda's World.**

Alston restructured it to suit the large playing field. He emphasized pitching and defense, and he utilized the stolen base more than any manager in decades.

While he mellowed with age, Alston never lost the respect of his players. "I know that as a handler of men, no one is better at it than Walt Alston," said Maury Wills. "He doesn't crack a whip or needle us. He treats us like men, and expects us to act that way."[6]

Alston led Los Angeles to World Series titles in 1959, 1963, and 1965. In his twenty-third and final season as Dodgers manager in 1976, he became the sixth manager ever to win two thousand games.

Tommy Lasorda

As a minor-league pitcher, Tommy Lasorda once struck out twenty-five batters in a 15-inning game. In 2000, he managed the United States baseball team to its first-ever Olympic gold medal. But what earned him induction to the Baseball Hall of Fame was his two decades of glory as manager of the Los Angeles Dodgers.

"I bleed Dodger blue," Lasorda beamed, "and when I die, I'm going to the big Dodger in the sky."[7]

From 1976 to 1996, Lasorda brought fun, hugs, and laughs to the Dodgers dugout. He knew baseball as well as any manager, but his enthusiasm and zest for the game set him apart. Even into his sixties, he was the team's biggest cheerleader. "Guys ask me, don't I get burned out?" he said. "How can you get burned out doing something you love? I ask you, have you ever got tired of kissing a pretty girl?"[8]

As Dodgers manager, Lasorda finished in first or second place in the NL West twelve times. He led the team to four World Series, which he won in 1981 and 1988. Twice he was named NL Manager of the Year.

Dodgers broadcaster Vin Scully covered many of the greatest games in baseball history from 1950 to 2006. The American Sportscasters Association selected him as the greatest sportscaster of the twentieth century.

⊜Vin Scully

Dodgers fans know the Vin Scully home run call by heart. "Swung on, a high drive to deep right field. Back goes Jackson, way back, to the wall . . . she's gone!"

From 1950 through 2006, eleven United States presidents came and went, but Vin Scully remained a constant. Scully has been described as baseball's poet laureate. Through vivid description and melodic tones, he captures the rhythm and essence of the sport. Said broadcaster Dick Enberg, "He paints the picture more beautifully than anyone who's ever called a baseball game."[9]

Scully joined the Dodgers shortly after graduating from Fordham University. He went on to broadcast more than eight thousand Dodgers games, plus a record twenty-eight World Series on television and radio. In 1988, he called Kirk Gibson's game-winning Series homer on NBC-TV.

In 1982, Scully earned a star on the Hollywood Walk of Fame. He was also voted "Sportscaster of the Century" by the American Sportscasters Association. Dodgers great Sandy Koufax paid him the ultimate compliment: "I enjoyed listening to Vin call a game almost more than playing in them."[10]

In 2006, Scully entered the final year of his contract with the Dodgers. Heaven help the broadcaster who will have to fill his shoes.

This young Dodgers fan waits patiently to get autographs before the Dodgers opening day game in 1992.

WELCOME TO DODGER STADIUM

In 1957, Brooklyn Dodgers owner Walter O'Malley negotiated with Los Angeles officials about moving his team to that city. Initially, the Dodgers would play in the Los Angeles Memorial Coliseum, a football stadium. But O'Malley wanted to build his own ballpark just for his team.

One day, O'Malley and a county supervisor took a helicopter ride over Los Angeles in search of potential stadium sites. O'Malley was intrigued with Chavez Ravine, a 300-acre lot surrounded by expressways with views of downtown. "Can I have that one?" O'Malley asked. "No problem," replied the supervisor.[1]

For decades, Chavez Ravine had been a tight-knit Mexican-American community. But in 1950, the city informed all residents that they had to sell their homes and move. Officials wanted to level the area, calling it an eyesore. Public housing was supposed to be built on the land, but that never materialized. Instead, it became the home for Dodger Stadium. After removing the last few families, ballpark construction began in September 1959. On April 10, 1962, Dodger Stadium officially opened.

Pretty and Clean

Thanks to the wealthy O'Malley, Dodger Stadium became the first privately funded major-league ballpark since Yankee Stadium in the 1920s. The original design called for a huge fountain behind the center-field fence, but that idea was eventually scrapped. Dodger Stadium would not have all the quirky features of Brooklyn's Ebbets Field, but it was a beautiful park that gleamed in the California sunshine.

Since fifty-two thousand fans arrived on Opening Day 1962, Dodger Stadium has changed little. The five-level structure features a multicolored seating bowl. Except for single-level seats, the outfield is open to breathtaking views: palm trees and rolling hills in the foreground and the San Gabriel Mountains in the distance. While walking the concourses, fans can see the downtown skyline.

Dodger Stadium has long been a "pitcher's park." The outfield fences are far away, making it difficult to hit home runs there. Both foul lines are 330 feet away. While the center-field fence is a

CHAVEZ RAVINE: A Los Angeles Story

Beneath Dodger Stadium lies a lost village...

Home to generations of Mexican Americans, Chavez Ravine was a close-knit village just miles from downtown Los Angeles. But in the 1950s, the city forcefully evicted the area's residents, razing their homes to make room for a new baseball stadium.

CHAVEZ RAVINE brings to life a neighborhood lost to corruption, city politics and corporate greed.

In 1957, the Dodgers were slated to leave New York for California, but they needed a place to play. Government officials offered to let the owners build on land close to downtown Los Angeles. Learn more about the destruction of Chavez Ravine on the **Chavez Ravine: A Los Angeles Story** Web site.

modest 395 feet, left-center and right-center are each a formidable 385. Moreover, the stadium's large foul territory translates into a lot of frustrating foul-outs by batters. The ballpark also boasts distinctive reddish dirt on the infield, warning track, and foul territory. Seventy percent of this dirt is actually red building brick crushed to a powder.

Since its inception, Dodger Stadium has been known as the cleanest ballpark in baseball. Workers give the place a hearty scrub-down, and the stadium is repainted every year. The outdoor grounds are beautifully landscaped, and ushers and stadium workers are especially courteous. The stadium may not be as high-tech as other ball-parks, but it does boast DodgerVision in left field. At 26′6″ x 46′6″, DodgerVision is the largest video screen in the majors.

Organist Nancy Bea Hefley has become a Dodgers legend. Traditionalists bemoan how rock and hip-hop have cut into her playing time. However, she still plays "Take Me Out to the Ballgame" during the seventh-inning stretch—a highlight of the Dodger Stadium experience.

⊝ Get Out Your Wallet

Dodgers tickets are pricey, although not as bad as at other major-league parks. The Dodgers offer fourteen types of tickets, with the most expensive being Field Box MVP (seventy-five dollars in 2006, if purchased in advance) and Infield Box (sixty-five dollars). Those on a budget can buy eight-dollar Pavilion seats behind the outfield fences. Fans also can purchase six-dollar Top Deck tickets behind home plate (binoculars are not included). All other tickets in 2006 ranged from twelve to fifty dollars.

Like Fenway Franks in Boston, Dodger Dogs have become part of baseball legend. In 2005, Dodgers fans consumed more than 1.6 million of them, at $3.50 each. The foot-long, all-pork wieners are grilled and wrapped in steamed buns. Vendors offer all sorts of food options, including nachos, veggie dogs, garlic fries, burritos, and pizza—not to mention peanuts and boxes of Cracker Jack!

Fans can buy Dodgers merchandise in and around the ballpark. The Top of the Park Store, located on the ninth level of Dodger Stadium, boasts a huge selection of goods. Of course, nothing is cheap. Dodger caps can top twenty dollars, jerseys one hundred dollars, and jackets two hundred dollars. Nevertheless, the team has never had trouble selling its products. There is something appealing about that sky blue—or as they call it in Los Angeles, "Dodger blue."

Renovations at Dodger Stadium, including DodgerVison, are meant to create a more interactive relationship between the team and the fans. Find out the details here, at the **Dodger Stadium Goes High-Tech** Web site.

⬅ The Game Experience

Over the years, Dodgers fans have been criticized for arriving late to games and leaving early. But it is not because Los Angelenos do not care about their team. Like all of Los Angeles, traffic to the ballpark is brutal, and parking is no picnic, either. Traveling the final mile to the parking lot, and then finding a space, can take a good forty-five minutes. Dodgers fans, however, do know their baseball. Middle-aged patrons grew up with the great Tommy Lasorda teams of the 1970s and

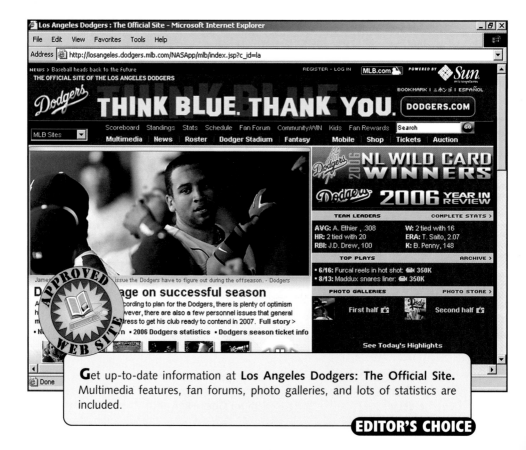

Get up-to-date information at **Los Angeles Dodgers: The Official Site.** Multimedia features, fan forums, photo galleries, and lots of statistics are included.

EDITOR'S CHOICE

early 1980s, and they have "bled Dodger blue" ever since. Many diehards listen to Vin Scully on the radio while watching the action.

Some games feel more like a day at the ocean, as fans like to whack beach balls around the stands. Also, daytime games in the summertime can be fiendishly hot. "For summer games bring sunscreen and maybe even a portable fan/spray bottle!" recommended one fan. "You WILL bake! And there have been instances that the park has run out of water!"[2] In the evenings, though, Dodger Stadium can be pure heaven. Soft, cooling breezes waft through the upper decks, while the setting sun illuminates the San Gabriel Mountains.

Following the Dodgers

In 1976, Dodgers fans voted broadcaster Vin Scully as the "Most Memorable Personality" in Los Angeles Dodgers history. Thirty years later, Scully remained the "Voice of the Dodgers." In fact, the Dodgers press box is named after him. In poll after poll, the articulate Scully is hailed as the greatest broadcaster in American sports history.

Rick Monday joined the Dodgers broadcasting team in 1993. As a former major-league outfielder, Monday provides keen insight as the color commentator. Many fans will never forget his heroics as a Chicago Cub in 1976. On April 25, two protesters were about to set the American flag ablaze in left field. Monday, a former member of the Marines Reserves, dashed toward the scene and swiped the flag before it burned.

More than 10 million Hispanic Americans live in California, and many of them love Jaime Jarrin. The "Spanish Voice of the Dodgers" has broadcast Dodgers games since 1959. Known for his smooth, melodic voice, Jarrin won the prestigious Ford C. Frick Award in 1998. Other Dodgers broadcasters include Steve "Psycho" Lyons, Pepe Yñiguez, and Fernando Valenzuela—the Dodgers pitcher who inspired "Fernandomania" in 1981.

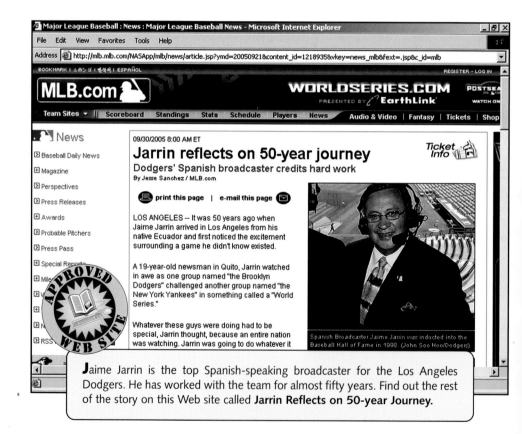

Jaime Jarrin is the top Spanish-speaking broadcaster for the Los Angeles Dodgers. He has worked with the team for almost fifty years. Find out the rest of the story on this Web site called **Jarrin Reflects on 50-year Journey.**

Like every major-league team, the Dodgers host their own Web site. Fans can read the latest information on their favorite players, check updated statistics, and even follow games in progress. The multimedia section is ever evolving. The site also includes a kids link. Young fans can play online baseball games and check out the latest Dodgers bobblehead or Pez dispenser.

⊜ Kid Friendly

The Dodgers realize the need to attract young fans—ones who will support the team throughout their lives. In 2006, kids could become free members of the Blue Crew, available through the Dodgers official Web site. A member receives a discounted ticket coupon as well as free prizes, such as a Blue Crew camera or an Eric Gagne paintable action figure. For a fee, kids could join the All-Star Blue Crew. Members receive such special prizes as a Universal Studios kids pass, a Dodgers messenger bag, and even a birthday card from Eric Gagne. Who could resist!

The Dodgers also host Kids Days at the ballpark. Lucky winners serve briefly as a public address announcer, grounds crew member, or on-field photographer. By catering to the little fans, the Dodgers hope to pack the stadium over the next generation—and beyond.

Pee Wee Reese was the Dodgers shortstop for many years. Aside from being a perennial all-star, Reese also is credited for standing up for teammate Jackie Robinson when Robinson needed support.

DODGER HEROES

Throughout their storied history, the Brooklyn/Los Angeles Dodgers have fielded nearly one hundred all-stars and more than forty Hall of Famers. Here is a look at some of the most memorable players in the history of the franchise.

⊖ Zack Wheat

In the early 1920s, a New York newspaper asked readers to pick the city's most popular player. Fans could have chosen Babe Ruth, but instead they selected Brooklyn's Zack Wheat.

Though almost entirely forgotten today, Wheat was the greatest Dodgers player of the first quarter of the twentieth century. From 1909 to 1926, he manned left field for Brooklyn. For years, a sign on Ebbets Field's outfield wall declared: "Zack Wheat caught 300 flies last year; Tanglefoot flypaper caught 10 million."[1]

Wheat patrolled the outfield gracefully, but his hitting earned him enshrinement in the Baseball Hall of Fame. Fourteen times he ripped over .300, and in 1918 he won the NL batting title (.335). In both 1923 and 1924, he stroked .375. To this day, Wheat holds the Dodgers record for career hits with 2,804.

Pee Wee Reese

Harold Reese was so small (five feet nine inches) and boyish looking, everyone called him "Pee Wee." Yet in baseball annals, he is one of the giants of the game. Reese was selected to ten All-Star teams and played in seven World Series for the Dodgers, and he is enshrined in the Baseball Hall of Fame.

A slick-fielding shortstop, Pee Wee also contributed offensively. In various seasons, he led the National League in walks, stolen bases, sacrifice bunts, and runs scored. But his greatest accomplishment came as team captain in 1947.

One day in Cincinnati, Reds players criticized Reese for playing with an African American. Pee Wee promptly put his arm around Jackie Robinson for thousands to see. Recalled Dodgers pitcher Rex Barney, it was "as if to say, 'This is my boy. This is the guy. We're gonna win with him.' "[2]

Recalled Robinson's wife, Rachel Robinson, "Pee Wee used all of his leadership skills and

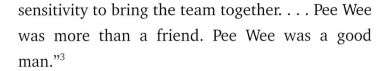

sensitivity to bring the team together. . . . Pee Wee was more than a friend. Pee Wee was a good man."[3]

Jackie Robinson

In 1945, Dodgers General Manager Branch Rickey intended on fielding the first black big-leaguer in the twentieth century. He needed an African American with exceptional talent and character. He needed Jackie Robinson.

Robinson served in the Army and attended UCLA, where he starred on the baseball, basketball, and

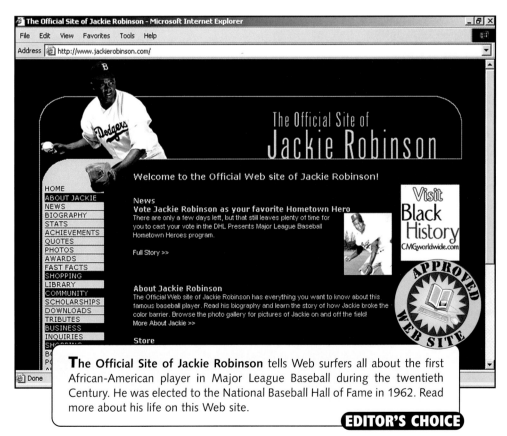

The Official Site of Jackie Robinson tells Web surfers all about the first African-American player in Major League Baseball during the twentieth Century. He was elected to the National Baseball Hall of Fame in 1962. Read more about his life on this Web site.

EDITOR'S CHOICE

Catcher Roy Campanella was named Most Valuable Player of the National League three times in his career. Sadly, Campanella was paralyzed as the result of injuries he sustained in a 1958 car accident.

football teams. In track, he broke the national record in the long jump. In October 1945, Robinson signed with the Dodgers—but only after promising he would "turn the other cheek" if physically or verbally assaulted.

As a rookie first baseman, Robinson endured a barrage of insults, hard tags, and beanballs. He retaliated only with magnificent play. Robinson led the league in steals (29) and scored 125 runs, winning the Rookie of the Year award. As a second baseman in 1949, his 124 RBI and league-best .342 average earned him the NL MVP award.

Robinson played ten seasons with Brooklyn, batting .300 six times. In 1997, in a move unprecedented in major-league history, acting Commissioner Bud Selig ordered that Robinson's No. 42 be retired by every major-league team.

Roy Campanella

To play baseball for a living, Roy Campanella said, "you have to have a lot of little boy in you."[4]

Of African-American and Italian descent, Campanella proved his toughness in the Negro Leagues. Players played injured, he said, "because if you didn't, you didn't get paid."[5] In 1948, "Campy" became the first Negro League catcher to play in the major leagues.

Behind the plate, Campanella displayed a rocket arm, strong leadership, and a great rapport with his pitchers. Offensively, the five-foot eight-inch slugger blasted thunderous home runs. His 41 homers and 142 RBI in 1953 set National League records for a catcher. Three times he was honored as NL MVP.

On January 29, 1958, Campanella's car skidded on ice and overturned. The accident left him paralyzed in his arms and legs. On May 7, 1959, at the Los Angeles Coliseum, more than ninety-three thousand fans honored Campanella—one of the most beloved Dodgers of all time.

Duke Snider

In the 1950s, fans of each New York team took pride in their center fielders: Willie Mays of the New York Giants, Mickey Mantle of the Yankees, and Duke Snider of the Dodgers. Wrote Red Smith, "You could get a fat lip in any saloon by starting an argument as to which was best."[6] Brooklyn fans had statistics to back them up: In the 1950s, Snider amassed more home runs (326) and RBI (1,031) than any other player in the major leagues.

"The Duke" adored Ebbets Field, especially its small dimensions. Beginning in 1953, Snider clubbed at least 40 home runs for five seasons in a row. He batted .341 in 1954, led the league in RBI in 1955 (136), and topped the NL in longballs in 1956 (43). His eleven career homers in World Series action remain an NL record.

Alas, Snider never adjusted to the move to Los Angeles. After his fifth 40-dinger season in 1957, he mustered just 15 in his first year in Los Angeles. Said the Duke: "When they tore down Ebbets Field, they tore down a little piece of me."[7]

Gil Hodges

When Gil Hodges slumped in early 1953, Brooklyn fans showed their love. They sent him letters of

▲ *The 1953 Dodgers infield included some of the best players at each position. Pictured left to right are Gil Hodges, Jim "Junior" Gilliam, Pee Wee Reese, and Jackie Robinson.*

encouragement, good-luck charms—even rosaries. Hodges finished the season with 122 RBIs.

A strong, silent type, Hodges manned first base for the Dodgers from 1948 to 1961. He drove in more than 100 runs for seven straight seasons, and he averaged 31 homers a year throughout the 1950s. On August 31, 1950, he blasted 4 home runs in one game.

With huge hands and quick feet, Hodges was a whiz at first base. He won a Gold Glove in 1957 (the first year it was awarded), then repeated in 1958 and 1959. All told, Hodges was selected to eight All-Star teams and played in seven World Series.

Hodges brought more joy to New York in 1969, when he managed the "Miracle Mets" to the world title. Three years later, he died at age forty-seven. Once again, New Yorkers sent their prayers.

Sandy Koufax

In 1953, Sandy Koufax left his home in Brooklyn for the University of Cincinnati, where he would play on the basketball team. He never dreamed he would be back in Brooklyn a year and a half later—as a Dodgers pitcher.

Koufax struggled with his control his first few seasons in the majors. But by 1962, everything clicked. The lefty repeatedly hit his targets with his blazing heater and sharp-breaking curveball.

Left-handed fireballer Sandy Koufax played only twelve seasons in the major leagues. But his last four seasons were some of the greatest ever produced by a pitcher.

Said Pittsburgh Pirates slugger Willie Stargell, "Trying to hit him was like trying to drink coffee with a fork."[8]

Over a five-year period, Koufax may have been the greatest pitcher of all time. From 1962 to 1966, he went 111–34 and led the league in ERA every season. In 1965, he set the major-league record for strikeouts with 382.

Koufax won three Cy Young Awards and the 1963 NL MVP award. He shone even brighter in the World Series, posting a 0.95 ERA in eight games. He set a big-league record with 4 no-hitters, including a perfect game in 1965. Koufax retired at age thirty due to injury, and six years later he became the youngest person ever elected to the Baseball Hall of Fame.

Don Drysdale

He was a hitter's worst nightmare. A six-foot six-inch giant with a menacing glare, Don Drysdale fired rockets to home plate. Moreover, he put hitters on edge with high, inside fastballs. Often, to show he was in charge, he hit batters on purpose. His 154 career hit batsmen remains a National League record. "The trick against Drysdale," said Giants slugger Orlando Cepeda, "is to hit him before he hits you."[9]

Drysdale's brand of intimidation earned him a spot in the Hall of Fame. From 1957 to 1968, he won at least twelve games every year. In 1962, he went 25–9 and won his third strikeout crown, earning the MLB Cy Young Award. Drysdale not only won twenty-three games in 1965, but he also batted .300 and socked 7 home runs.

Drysdale's final burst of glory came in 1968. Amazingly, he authored 6 straight shutouts and set a major-league record with 58 consecutive scoreless innings. A blown shoulder ended his career at age thirty-three.

Ace pitcher Don Drysdale used his menacing stare to intimidate opposing hitters.

Maury Wills

In the 1950s, teams relied on home runs and the "big inning" to win ballgames. The stolen base had become passé. Then along came Maury Wills.

A slightly built shortstop for the Dodgers, Wills did not possess blazing speed. However, he took daring leads at first base, and by studying each pitcher he learned the exact moment when to break for second. Wills led the NL in steals as a rookie in 1960 (50) and in 1961 (35). The following season, he ran hog wild.

In 1962, Wills became the first big leaguer in modern history to steal 100 bases in a season. He broke Ty Cobb's major-league record of 96, and he finished with 104. The Giants were so desperate to slow him down that they watered the dirt around first base so he could not get a quick jump. San Francisco won the pennant, but Wills was named NL MVP.

Wills's amazing season revolutionized the game. Soon, every team was looking for a dynamic base thief. But no one in the National League could match Wills. He led the circuit in steals for six straight seasons, including 94 in 1965.

Don Sutton

Don Sutton never won the Cy Young Award, and only once did he win twenty games. But year after year—for seventeen straight seasons—he won at

Don Sutton was a consistent winner during his twenty-three seasons of big-league pitching for five teams. His best years, the ones that earned him a Hall of Fame induction, were with the Dodgers.

least eleven games. "[T]o me it's like a routine thing," he said, "like going to the office or walking into a factory."[10]

What Sutton produced were victories. From 1969 through 1976, he averaged eighteen wins a year. He mixed his pitches masterfully, throwing fastballs, curveballs, sliders, and change-ups. Thirteen times he ranked among the league's top ten in strikeouts.

From his "office," the pitcher's mound, Sutton toiled for twenty-three years. His totals were staggering: 324 victories and 3,574 strikeouts. These numbers earned him enshrinement in the Baseball Hall of Fame. Moreover, with 233 victories for Los Angeles, he reigns as the winningest pitcher in Dodgers history.

Steve Garvey

"Mr. Perfect," they called him, and he fit the description in many ways. Well groomed with chiseled features, Steve Garvey looked dapper in his Dodgers uniform. Off the field, he acted like a gentleman and always had time for autographs. "You sign a baseball for a kid," Garvey explained, "and you've done something he's going to carry with him for years."[11]

From 1975 to 1983, Garvey had perfect attendance: He played in a National League-record 1,207 consecutive games. At the plate, he took

Steve Garvey was a fan favorite and excellent first baseman. Some players, though, resented the attention he received for seemingly being a clean-cut guy.

crisp, clean cuts. In 1984, he did not make an error all year.

Garvey's "good guy" image sometimes aggravated his teammates. However, everyone loved his production. From 1974 to 1980, he totaled 100 RBIs five times, 200 hits six times, and a .300 average six times. In every one of those seasons, he was selected to play in the All-Star Game. As All-Star voters saw it, he was the perfect choice.

Fernando Valenzuela

In the spring of 1981, "Fernandomania" swept across Southern California. The little-known rookie fired a shutout on Opening Day, then won his next seven starts! Fans had never seen such pitching dominance. Along with his 8–0 record, Valenzuela tossed 5 shutouts while posting an unheard-of 0.50 ERA. Over one stretch, he threw 36 straight scoreless innings.

One of the few Mexican players in the majors, the twenty-year-old rookie thrilled Hispanic-American fans. The stocky lefty also boasted a mesmerizing delivery. During his windup,

Valenzuela twisted slightly backward, briefly closed his eyes, and then unloaded. Valenzuela was one of the few ever to master the screwball. This pitch actually breaks in the opposite direction of all other breaking balls.

Valenzuela finished the strike-shortened 1981 season 13–7 with a 2.48 ERA. He won the NL Cy Young Award and Rookie of the Year Award. He even copped the Silver Slugger award as the NL's best hitting pitcher.

Valenzuela made the All-Star team for six straight seasons. He peaked in 1986, winning twenty-one games as well as a Gold Glove for his fielding excellence.

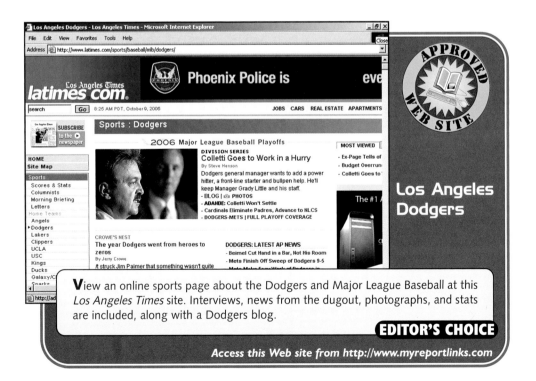

View an online sports page about the Dodgers and Major League Baseball at this *Los Angeles Times* site. Interviews, news from the dugout, photographs, and stats are included, along with a Dodgers blog.

EDITOR'S CHOICE

Access this Web site from http://www.myreportlinks.com

Mike Piazza is arguably the best hitting catcher in baseball history. He produced some of his best seasons while playing for the Dodgers.

Mike Piazza

In the 1988 amateur baseball draft, the Dodgers selected catcher Mike Piazza way down in the sixty-second round. And that was only because Piazza's father was friends with Dodgers manager Tommy Lasorda. No one expected the teenager to make the major leagues—let alone become the greatest hitting catcher of all time.

In five years in the minors, Piazza spent endless hours in the batting cage and weight room. The hard work paid off in 1993. Piazza batted .318 with 35 homers and 112 RBI for the Dodgers, winning the NL Rookie of the Year Award.

In his five full seasons with Los Angeles, Piazza averaged 33 homers and 105 RBI, along with a .337 batting average. He amazed fans with his immense power to the opposite field. In one game, he hit a ball completely out of Dodger Stadium.

Los Angeles traded Mike Piazza in 1998, but he continued to hammer the ball. He won ten straight Silver Slugger awards as the NL's top-hitting catcher. In 2006, he became the first catcher ever to belt 400 home runs.

Eric Gagne

In 2001, Eric Gagne made 24 starts for Los Angeles and won just 6 games. In 2002, the Dodgers demoted him to the bullpen—and a star was born.

Gagne possessed the "killer instinct" to excel as the team's closer. He also packed a 98-mph fast-ball as well as a "vulcan" change-up. Spreading his index and middle fingers like a *Star Trek* "V," Gagne made his pitch drop at the last instant. With these pitches and newfound control, he became virtually unhittable.

In 2002, Gagne recorded 52 saves—five shy of the major-league record. The next season, he won the NL Cy Young Award after achieving an unprecedented feat: He earned 55 saves in fifty-five chances. That meant he did not blow a lead all year. In 82 $^2/_3$ innings, he yielded just 37 hits and logged a 1.20 ERA. Not until July 2004 did Gagne give up the lead, ending his record streak of 84 consecutive saves.

Who will be the Dodgers' stars of the future?

Report Links

The Internet sites described below can be accessed at http://www.myreportlinks.com

▶**Los Angeles Dodgers: The Official Site**
Editor's Choice Visit this official site for news of the team.

▶**Los Angeles Dodgers**
Editor's Choice This site offers complete coverage of the L.A. Dodgers.

▶**National Baseball Hall of Fame and Museum**
Editor's Choice Visit this museum site to learn more about the game of baseball.

▶**Gibson Delivers in a Pinch**
Editor's Choice Read about one of baseball's "twenty-five greatest moments."

▶**The Official Site of Jackie Robinson**
Editor's Choice Biographical info and photos of Jackie Robinson.

▶**Walter O'Malley Official Website**
Editor's Choice Learn more about the Dodger owner when you visit this Web site.

▶**Baseball As America**
The National Baseball Hall of Fame and Museum presents this baseball exhibition Web site.

▶**The Baseball Biography Project**
Major league player biographies are available on this site.

▶**Baseball Cards 1887–1914**
The Library of Congress has posted images of 2,100 early baseball cards.

▶**Chavez Ravine: A Los Angeles Story**
PBS looks at how the village of Chavez Ravine ended up buried under Dodger Stadium.

▶**Da Bums of Summer**
Test your knowledge of the Dodgers when you take this trivia quiz.

▶**Dodgers Capture 1st World Series; Podres Wins, 2–0**
The Brooklyn Dodgers and the New York Yankees battled it out in 1955.

▶**Dodger Stadium Goes High-Tech**
Take a look at DodgerVision.

▶**Dodger Stadium/Los Angeles Dodgers**
Facts, figures, and a history of Dodger Stadium.

▶**Ebbets Field**
This site has the facts, figures, and photographs for historic Ebbets Field.

Report Links

The Internet sites described below can be accessed at
http://www.myreportlinks.com

▶**Fernando Valenzuela**
Get the facts on pitcher and broadcaster Fernando Valenzuela.

▶**Giants-Dodgers Covers a Lot of Ground**
A *Washington Post* article on the history of the rivalry between the Dodgers and Giants.

▶**Green is 14th to Hit Four HRs in a Game**
This ESPN article focuses on Shawn Green.

▶**Higher Calling**
Explore the other side of Branch Rickey.

▶**An In-Depth Look at Dodger Stadium's Effects**
This article looks at how players and the game of baseball are interconnected with ballpark design.

▶**Jarrin Reflects on 50-year Journey**
This MLB.com article is about award-winning broadcaster, Jaime Jarrin.

▶**Los Angeles Dodgers (1958–Present)**
Visit this Web site for Los Angeles Dodgers history.

▶**1988 World Series**
Official stats of the 1988 World Series.

▶**The Official Site of Carl Erskine**
A biography of Carl Erskine, with quotes, photos, and pitching highlights.

▶**Orel Hershiser**
Bio and statistics for Dodgers pitcher Orel Hershiser.

▶**Salaries Database**
Check major league ballplayer salaries on this Web site.

▶**Sandy Koufax: Baseball Legend**
This BBC article takes a look at Sandy Koufax.

▶**Science of Baseball**
The Exploratorium Museum explores the science of baseball.

▶**Society for American Baseball Research**
SABR is dedicated to the study of baseball.

▶**Tommy Lasorda's World**
Visit Tommy Lasorda's baseball blog.

Career

MVP AWARD WINNERS	YEAR	AVG	HR	RBI
Jake Daubert*	1913	.350	2	52
Dazzy Vance**	1924	Pitcher, 28–6, 2.16 ERA		
Dolph Camilli	1941	.285	34	120
Jackie Robinson	1949	.342	16	124
Roy Campanella	1951	.325	33	108
Roy Campanella	1953	.312	41	142
Roy Campanella	1955	.318	32	107
Don Newcombe	1956	Pitcher, 27–7, 3.06 ERA		
Maury Wills	1962	.299	6	48
Sandy Koufax	1963	Pitcher, 25–5, 1.88 ERA		
Steve Garvey	1974	.312	21	111
Kirk Gibson	1988	.290	25	76

*From 1911–14 the MVP Award was known as the Chalmers Award
**From 1922–29 the MVP Award was known as the League Award

CY YOUNG AWARD WINNERS*	YEAR	W	L	ERA
Don Newcombe	1956	27	7	3.06
Don Drysdale	1962	25	9	2.83
Sandy Koufax	1963	25	5	1.88
Sandy Koufax	1965	26	8	2.04
Sandy Koufax	1966	27	9	1.73
Mike Marshall	1974	15	12	2.42 (21 saves)
Fernando Valenzuela	1981	13	7	2.48
Orel Hershiser	1988	23	8	2.26
Eric Gagne	2003	2	3	1.20 (55 saves)

*Cy Young Award first presented in 1956

Stats

PLAYER	YRS	G	AB	R	H	HR	RBI	SB	AVG
Roy Campanella	10	1,215	4,205	627	1,161	242	856	25	.276
Ron Cey	17	2,073	7,162	977	1,868	316	1,139	24	.261
Steve Garvey	19	2,332	8,835	1,143	2,559	272	1,308	83	.294
Kirk Gibson	17	1,635	5,798	985	1,553	255	870	284	.268
Gil Hodges	18	2,071	7,030	1,105	1,921	370	1,274	63	.273
Davey Lopes	16	1,812	6,354	1,023	1,671	155	614	557	.263
Mike Piazza	15	1,829	6,602	1,015	2,042	419	1,291	17	.309
Pee Wee Reese	16	2,166	8,058	1,338	2,170	126	885	232	.269
Jackie Robinson	10	1,382	4,877	947	1,518	137	734	197	.311
Duke Snider	18	2,143	7,161	1,259	2,116	407	1,333	99	.295
Zack Wheat	19	2,410	9,106	1,289	2,884	132	1,248	205	.317
Maury Wills	14	1,942	7,588	1,067	2,134	20	458	586	.281

PLAYER	YRS	G	IP	W	L	SV	SO	SHO	ERA
Don Drysdale	14	518	3,432.0	209	166	6	2,486	49	2.95
Eric Gagne	8	298	545.3	25	21	161	629	0	3.27
Orel Hershiser	18	510	3,130.3	204	150	5	2,014	25	3.48
Mike Marshall	14	723	1,386.7	97	112	188	880	1	3.14
Don Newcombe	10	344	2,154.7	149	90	7	1,129	24	3.56
Sandy Koufax	12	397	2,324.7	165	87	9	2,396	40	2.76
Don Sutton	23	774	5,282.3	324	256	5	3,574	58	3.26
Fernando Valenzuela	17	453	2,930.0	173	153	2	2,074	31	3.54

American Association—A defunct major league that operated from 1882–91. Should not be confused with a minor league by the same name.

backdoor slider—A hard breaking ball that starts outside of the plate but comes back over the outer edge.

commissioner—The person in charge of Major League Baseball, as appointed by the owners.

Cy Young Award—An award given each year to the best pitcher in each major league.

"Dem Bums"—Nickname for the Dodgers from the 1930s through 1954.

dinger—Another word for a home run.

Dodger Stadium—Home of the L.A. Dodgers since 1962; located in Los Angeles, California.

donnybrook—In sports, an exciting game.

Ebbets Field—Home of the Brooklyn Dodgers that was demolished in 1960.

ERA—Earned run average. The average number of earned runs a pitcher gives up per nine innings.

fireballer—A pitcher who is known for throwing hard fastballs.

Gold Glove—Annual award given to the best fielding player at each position.

homer—Another word for a home run.

Major League Baseball Players Association—A union that represents all of the baseball players in the major leagues.

Most Valuable Player—Annual award given to the player who the Baseball Writers Association of America (BBWAA) feels most helped his team succeed.

National League—One of baseball's two major leagues; the other is the American League.

Negro League—A baseball league in which African-American players performed before they were allowed into Major League Baseball.

no-hitter—A game in which a pitcher does not surrender a base hit.

pennant—A league championship, alternately called the flag.

perfect game—A game in which a pitcher does not allow anyone on the opposing team to reach base.

preseason—Spring training practices and games that begin about a month before opening day.

Rookie of the Year Award—An annual award given out since 1947 to that season's best first-year player. Since 1949, it was been awarded to one player in each league.

shutout—When a pitcher pitches a complete game without allowing a run.

slugger—A powerful hitter known for blasting homers and driving in runs.

Subway Series—An event that occurs when the two New York teams play each other in the World Series.

Chapter 1. "I Don't Believe What I Just Saw!"

1. Kirk Gibson with Lynn Henning, *Bottom of the Ninth* (Farmington Hills, Mich.: Sleeping Bear Press, 1997), p. 130.

2. Ibid., p. 131.

3. Ken Gurnick, "Gibson hits a true walk-off homer," *mlb.com,* August 7, 2002, <http://mlb.mlb .com/NASApp/mlb/mlb/news/mlb_news.jsp?ymd=20 020807&content_id=98677&vkey=news_mlb&fext= .jsp> (January 26, 2006).

4. Gibson, *Bottom of the Ninth,* p. 131.

5. "A hobbled Gibson homers in a pinch," *mlb.com,* October 15, 1988, <http://mlb.mlb.com/NASApp /mlb/mlb/baseballs_best/mlb_bb_gamepage.jsp?story _page=bb_88ws_gm1_oakla> (January 27, 2006).

6. Ibid.

7. "Gibson Delivers in a Pinch," *SportingNews,* n.d., <http://archive.sportingnews.com/baseball/25moments /6.html> (January 27, 2006).

8. "A hobbled Gibson homers in a pinch," *mlb.com,* October 15, 1988, <http://mlb.mlb.com/NASApp/mlb /mlb/baseballs_best/mlb_bb_gamepage.jsp?story_ page=bb_88ws_gm1_oakla> (January 27, 2006).

9. Ken Gurnick, "Gibson hits a true walk-off homer," *mlb.com,* August 7, 2002, <http://mlb.mlb .com/NASApp/mlb/mlb/news/mlb_news.jsp?ymd= 20020807&content_id=98677&vkey=news_mlb&fext= .jsp> (January 26, 2006).

Chapter 2. The Bums of Brooklyn

1. "Willie Keeler quotes," *Thinkexist.com,* n.d., <http://en.thinkexist.com/quotation/hit-em-where- they-ain t/535843.html> (February 3, 2006).

2. "Dodgers Timeline," *mlb.com,* n.d., <http://losangeles.dodgers.mlb.com/NASApp/mlb/la/history/timeline05.jsp> (February 4, 2006).

3. "Ebbets Field," *Baseball-statistics.com,* n.d., <http://www.baseball statistics.com/Ballparks/LA/Ebbetts.htm> (February 4, 2006).

4. "Jackie Robinson Breaks Baseball's Color Barrier, 1945," *Eye Witness to History.com,* n.d., <http://www.eyewitnesstohistory.com/robinson.htm> (February 5, 2006).

5. "Frick, Ford," *HickockSports.com,* n.d., <http://www.hickoksports.com/quotes/quotef01.shtml> (February 6, 2006).

6. "The Shot Heard 'Round the World," *Sporting News,* n.d., <http://tsn.sportingnews.com/baseball/25moments/1.html> (February 6, 2006).

7. Paul Adomites *et al., The Golden Age of Baseball* (Lincolnwood, Ill.: Publications International, 2003), pp. 151–152.

8. Eric Enders, *1903–2004: 100 Years of the World Series* (New York: Sterling Publishing, 2003), p. 130.

9. Peter Golenbock, *Bums: An Oral History of the Brooklyn Dodgers* (New York: G. P. Putnam's Sons, 1984), p. 405.

10. Ibid., p. 407.

11. Ibid., p. 446.

Chapter 3. California Bound

1. Donald Honig, *The Los Angeles Dodgers: The First Quarter Century* (New York: St. Martin's Press, 1983), p. 2.

2. Gene Schoor, *The History of the World Series* (New York: William Morrow and Company, 1990), p. 284.

3. Honig, p. 55.

4. "Tommy Lasorda Los Angeles Dodgers," *LosAngelesDodgersOnline.com,* n.d., <http://www.losangelesdodgersonline.com/tommylasorda.php> (February 19, 2006).

Chapter 4. Mania and Miracles

1. Donald Honig, *The Los Angeles Dodgers: The First Quarter Century* (New York: St. Martin's Press, 1983), p. 140.

2. Orel Hershiser with Jerry B. Jenkins, *Out of the Blue* (Brentwood, Tenn.: Wolgemuth & Hyatt, Publishers, 1989), p. 207.

Chapter 5. The Masterminds

1. "Leo Durocher Quotes," *BrainyQuote,* n.d., <http://www.brainyquote.com/quotes/quotes/l/leoduroche111944.html> (February 26, 2006).

2. Ken Gurnick, "Robinson breaks the color barrier," *mlb.com,* July 24, 2002, <http://mlb.mlb.com/NASApp/mlb/mlb/news/mlb_news.jsp?ymd=20020724&content_id=88506&vkey=news_mlb&fext=.jsp> (February 26, 2006).

3. Ed Shakespeare, "Brooklyn's Southern tradition," *BrooklynPapers.com,* August 18, 2003, <http://www.brooklynpapers.com/html/cyclones/html/shakespeare/2003season/26_33plays.html> (February 28, 2006).

4. David Pietrusza, Matthew Silverman, Michael Gershman (editors), *Baseball: The Biographical Encyclopedia* (New York: Total/Sports Illustrated, 2000), p. 56.

5. Ibid., p. 938.

6. Ibid., p. 24.

7. "Tommy Lasorda Los Angeles Dodgers," *LosAngelesDodgersOnline.com,* n.d.,<http://www.losangelesdodgersonline.com/tommylasorda.php> (March 1, 2006).

8. "Tommy Lasorda Quotes," *BrainyQuote,* n.d., <http://www.brainyquote.com/quotes/authors/t/tommy_lasorda.html> (March 1, 2006).

9. Gary Kaufman, "Vin Scully," *Salon.com,* October 12, 1999, <http://www.salon.com/people/bc/1999/10/12/scully> (March 10, 2006).

10. Ben Platt, "A photo scrapbrook of Vin & The All Century Team in 1999," *mlb.com,* 2001–2006, <http://losangeles.dodgers.mlb.com/NASApp/mlb/la/history/vin_scully_tribute/all_century.jsp> (March 10, 2006).

Chapter 6. Welcome to Dodger Stadium

1. "Dodger Stadium," *ballparks.com,* n.d., <http://www.ballparks.com/baseball/national/dodger.htm> (March 12, 2006).

2. "Dodger Stadium Experiences," *Ballparks of Baseball,* n.d., <http://www.ballparksofbaseball.com/reviews/dodreviews.htm> (March 13, 2006).

Chapter 7. Dodger Heroes

1. David Pietrusza, *Baseball: The Biographical Encyclopedia* (New York: Total/Sports Illustrated, 2000), p. 1214.

2. Matthew Silverman, Michael Gershman (editors), "Pee Wee Reese," *Baseball Almanac,* n.d., <http://www.baseball almanac.com/quotes/pee_wee_reese_quotes.shtml> (March 15, 2006).

3. Ibid.

4. "Historical Photo Gallery," *RoyCampanella.com,* n.d., <http://www.roycampanella.com/quotes.htm> (March 15, 2006).

5. Pietrusza, p. 162.

6. "Jack Roosevelt Robinson," *Baseball-statistics.com,* n.d., <http://www.baseball-statistics.com/HOF/Robinson Jackie.html> (March 16, 2006).

7. Paul Dickson, *Baseball's Greatest Quotations* (New York: HarperCollins, 1991), p. 404.

8. "Sandy Koufax, " *Everything2,* n.d., <http ://www .everything2.com/index.pl?node=Sandy%20Koufax> (March 18, 2006).

9. "About Don Drysdale," *The Official Site of Don Drysdale,* n.d., <http://www.dondrysdale.com/about /quote.html> (March 19, 2006).

10. "Autograph of the Week," *Baseball Almanac,* n.d., <http://www.baseball-almanac.com/autoweek /auto9.shtml> (March 20, 2006).

11. Pietrusza, p. 401.

Allen, Maury. *Brooklyn Remembered: The 1955 Days of the Dodgers.* Champaign, Ill.: Sports Publishing, 2005.

Delsohn, Steve. *True Blue: The Dramatic History of the Los Angeles Dodgers, Told by the Men Who Lived It.* New York: Perennial Currents, 2002.

Golenbock, Peter. *Bums: An Oral History of the Brooklyn Dodgers.* Chicago: McGraw-Hill/Contemporary, 2000.

Grabowski, John F. *Los Angeles Dodgers.* San Diego: Lucent Books, 2003.

Hanft, Joshua E. *Jackie Robinson.* Edina, Minn.: Abdo Publishers, 2005.

Leavy, Jane. *Sandy Koufax: A Lefty's Legacy.* New York: HarperCollins, 2002.

McNeil, William F. *The Dodgers Encyclopedia.* Champaign, Ill.: Sports Publishing, 2003.

Pietrusza, David. *The Los Angeles Dodgers Baseball Team.* Springfield, N.J.: Enslow Publishers, Inc., 1999.

Stewart, Wayne. *The History of the Los Angeles Dodgers.* Mankato, Minn.: Creative Education, 2003.

Stout, Glenn and Richard A. Johnson. *The Dodgers: 120 Years of Dodgers Baseball.* Boston: Houghton Mifflin, 2004.

Whittingham, Richard. *Illustrated History of the Dodgers.* Chicago: Triumph Books, 2005.